MW01482517

FARMWIVES 2:

An Inspiring Look at the Lives of the New Canadian Farmwives

Pat :
Enjoy
the Stories
too,
bjm

BILLI J MILLER

 FriesenPress

Suite 300 - 990 Fort St
Victoria, BC, V8V 3K2
Canada

www.friesenpress.com

Author photograph and Book cover photograph by Brin Dyer (www.be-photography.ca).

For information about book discounts for bulk purchases, please contact the Author directly at: billi@billijmillerphotography.com

Author Website: www.billijmillerphotography.com

ISBN
978-1-5255-2187-4 (Hardcover)
978-1-5255-2188-1 (Paperback)
978-1-5255-2189-8 (eBook)

1. Biography & Autobiography, Women

Distributed to the trade by The Ingram Book Company

Contents

Dedication:

As always, to Dean, Madeline and Kate: I can't imagine a better life than with the three of you. You are my heart and soul.

To the girls (the group of seven): thank you for being my people. We are beyond lucky to have each other. Here's to thirty years together and counting...

Thanks to two writing teachers of mine that have bit by bit coaxed more heartfelt and honest writing out of me: Alexandra Franzen and Nancy Aronie. I'm so lucky to learn from the two of you. Thanks for seeing me and believing in me.

To Rebecca K—thank you for your heartfelt contribution that I know will help so many learn from your loss and heartache. I never intended for the "widow" piece to be provided by you. There are still great things for you in this world. You are strong, full of grace, and love. Walk tall.

To Edith P (Farmwife #1/Book #1)—you're in my heart forever...

Note from the Author:

* None of the opinions expressed in this book (including the professional contributions in the "food for thought" section) are to be taken as "advice". Please seek out your own professional advice when handling matters on your own family farm.

Nice Things People Have Said:

"Farm women are mentors and encouragers to others seeking to be fulfilled on the farm. We learn from each other's journey and stories, so enjoy this collection. Let these women fire up your passion and vision!"

Elaine Froese, Professional Speaker, Writer & Coach.
www.elainefroese.com

"I hope this is one of a hundred book series!"

Bridget Ryan, Producer/TV-Host Dinner Television (On Interview with Billi J. Miller about Farmwives in Profile: 17 Women, 17 Candid Questions about their Lives, Photos & Recipes
www.bridgetryan.com

"You are doing such good work on the world. Amen! Keep doing this. It is changing lives."

Lori Claerhout, Writer & Editor.
www.loriclaerhout.com

"You have really helped empower me at a time where I felt like I had no power left at all. I'm not sure if that was any of your intentions, but I do appreciate this gift."

Farmwives 2 Interviewee

Other Books by the Author:

Farmwives in Profile: 17 Women, 17 Candid Questions about their Lives, Photos & Recipes
FriesenPress Publishing, 2016.

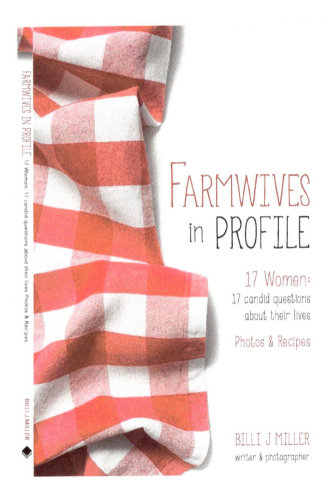

Prologue

FROM THE CITY TO A HUNDRED-YEAR-OLD PRAIRIE FARM:
THE AUTHOR'S STORY

I remember being told nearly ten years ago by my mentor, an Aboriginal Elder whom I worked with at the time, that my future would involve working with (and for) women. He must have seen what I hadn't yet myself seen, as a trail of passions soon followed, which included becoming the photographer for a march for missing and murdered women and fighting for the rights of aboriginal communities to safe drinking water. And now, although on the surface different—maybe at it's core, though, it's much the same—I am shining light on farm women for their remarkable contributions to not only their homes, families and farms—but, to Canada's cultural heritage, also.

"These women have been the pillars holding these communities up for a very long time and must be celebrated," I wrote in my first book on the subject.

I'm sure given my own life transition to becoming a farmwife, mother and business-owner myself (and trying to balance that) while being a "present" work-from-home-mom that makes me delve deeper into our places as women.

I have fallen deeply in love with farm life. In 2010, I married a fourth-generation farmer from East Central Alberta, Canada. We live on the original homestead that my husband's great-grandfather homesteaded in 1911. My husband's father was raised on this farm. Now we raise our two daughters here. There is a beautiful old barn in the backyard that I look at every morning from my kitchen window. It makes me think about permanence and deep roots, and how very much those things now mean to me.

When I was growing up, my family spent a number of years living on a Saskatchewan farm on the Prairies as renters. My parents (who were not farmers) rented the house, and that is where our family lived. I was young, but I have memories of going on combine rides, watching the cows being milked (by hand), and playing in the upstairs of the old dairy barn. I still remember the smell of the old books that had been abandoned up there.

I also spent many Christmases at my aunt and uncle's farm near the border of Alberta and Saskatchewan, south of Lloydminster. I remember Boxing Day sleigh rides drawn by horses, skating on frozen sloughs, and lots of summer camping trips to the fish-rich lakes in Northern Saskatchewan.

Yet my junior and senior high school years and most of my adulthood were spent living in the city. At university I began a life in Calgary, Alberta, and I would spend a decade there. It began with my undergrad schooling, followed by years of trying out a number of jobs as I attempted to figure out what "career path" would be the best fit for me.

In 2004 I relocated to Edmonton, where I began a career in the provincial government. That would span five more years, which took me into my thirties, by which time I had happily settled into the thought that I may just be a "city girl" for life. So I thought, anyway …

ABOUT THE TIME I WENT FISHING AND SNAGGED A FARMER

In August 2009 I met my husband (whom I'd immediately and affectionately nicknamed "Farmer") while on a family fishing trip at a lake in Northern Saskatchewan.

I was visiting my aforementioned aunt and uncle that weekend, as they spent their summer at the lake. The Farmer, Dean Miller, was there with a mutual family friend. They both lived about twenty minutes outside of the city I grew up in. Dean and I hadn't known each other growing up; instead we met, on that fateful fishing trip, at the mutual age of thirty-four.

Dean and I spent a lot of time chatting around the campfire that weekend, learning about each other, our lives, and what we thought was important. We clicked. And at the end of the weekend, we exchanged numbers.

I returned to my city life in Edmonton, but soon I found myself spending a lot of time on his nearly-one-hundred-year-old family farm, two hours east of Edmonton. I tell myself that I dazzled him with my fishing skills, while his dreamy eyes had dazzled me. "I went fishing and snagged a farmer," is what I e-mailed to my best girlfriends when I told them about the experience.

TRADITION, ROOTS AND RELOCATING TO THE FARM

Dean Miller wasn't just any farmer. He's a born-in-a-plaid-shirt, sure-of-his-life's-path, never-questioned-where-he'd-spend-his-life kind of a farmer. It was fitting, then, that he lived on the old family farm's original homestead.

I had nothing close to such romantic roots. You see, my family life has been rocked by instability, divorce, and frequent moves over my childhood. Living on the land where your father himself grew up was a complete unknown for me.

Dean lived in his grandparents' old house, about a ten-minute drive from his parents' home. In April 2010, I was able to find a job within a forty-minute commute from the farm, and I moved there. In summer, while on a road trip to Alaska, Dean proposed, and we were married in October 2010. We were both thirty-five. As I settled into "life on the farm" it was not hard to immediately spot the unyielding dedication and tireless work ethic of the "farmwives" in this new home of mine.

Fast-forward to the time of writing, the winter of 2017: Dean and I live here with our two girls (six and four) in the same house and in our eighth year of marriage. We are happy. We work hard every day; he in his shop and doing the physical farm work, and I looking after our kids, our family's schedule, and running a growing business of my own that brings together photography, freelance writing, and book writing. We are enjoying our family, making memories, planning our future, and watching our girls grow.

Farmwives The First

You don't have to know me very long before you begin to see what I'm passionate about. I wear my heart on my sleeve, I always have. I dreamed of becoming a writer, photographer, and journalist since my elementary school years; since then I have created a profession for myself where I am doing two of those three things.

After having my first daughter, I decided it would be more worthwhile to start my own business than return to a desk job I felt unfulfilled at, so in 2012, I began a photography business in which my niche was photographing farm families. Soon after that, I began writing freelance for local newspapers also.

With my immersion into farm life it took no time at all before I became enamoured by the commitment, contributions, and dedication of the farmwives I met. These amazing women have dedicated their lives to the nurturing and successful running of their families, farms, and communities. Their tireless work ethic is staggering. So, too, is their humility. It is because of these remarkable qualities that I very quickly became passionate about shining a light on the scores of women who, I felt, held these farm communities up. Thus, the concept of my first book was born.

It took more than four years to write and publish a book entirely dedicated to this subject. *Farmwives in Profile: 17 Women, 17 Candid Questions about their Lives, Photos & Recipes* featured candid interviews with seventeen Canadian Prairie women between the ages of fifty-five and ninety. These profiles detailed their lives on their farms and included photos as well as over twenty traditional straight-from-the-farm-kitchen recipes. Two years after it's January 2016 release, I still continue to sing the praises of these unsung heroes of family farms at author events and conferences.

I live in the shadow of one such woman. My mother-in-law, Wendy Miller, raised four boys with her husband, Gary, a third-generation farmer. They've been married over forty years. Her work and dedication to her marriage, in her home, and for their family business is astounding and continues strong to this day. Much of her life, and certainly her day-to-day, is often planned around the feeding of her family. This extends far outside of harvest meals and translates to her being the dutiful cook daily for her husband and one adult son who continues to live with them. In addition to her role in her home and with their farm company, she is steadfast in her community involvement. Perhaps though most meaningful to me, Wendy is a dedicated, loving, always-counted-on Grandma to her grandchildren. And, for that, I could not be more grateful. My mother-in-law is a true pillar to this family.

I asked Wendy seventeen questions: the same questions that were asked of all the women in my first book. These are her answers.

Wendy Miller

1. How long have you lived in this community?

I moved to Paradise Valley, Alberta, in the fall of 1971 to teach at the Junior-Senior High School. I met Gary in the spring of 1972, married in June 1974, and settled on the farm in the Earlie District.

2. What was your background prior to marrying your husband?

I was raised in small-town Saskatchewan—in Parry—along with four brothers and two sisters. My dad was a Saskatchewan Wheat Pool Elevators agent. I graduated from Pangman High School, attended the University of Saskatchewan, Regina Campus, receiving a Bachelor of Education degree in spring 1971. Paradise Valley, Alberta, was where I got my first teaching job.

3. How long have you been married and how many children do you have?

I've been married forty-one years and have four children, Dean, Mike, Brad, and Craig. Dean married Billi and they have two daughters, Madeline and Kate. Mike married Stephanie and they have two boys, Dane and Aiden, and a girl, Sophia. Brad lives in nearby Lloydminster, and Craig lives with Gary and myself.

4. What has the role of farmwife meant to you?

As a wife, I became a housekeeper, a cook, a baker, a chauffeur, a mother, a gardener, a barber, and a volunteer. As a farmwife, I became a bookkeeper plus all of the above. It was my job to keep everything going, especially during the busy times of calving, seeding, and harvest. I became very independent and organized. I learned to do a lot of things on my own—always knowing I could be called on at any time to drop everything and go help the men!

Now as we approach retirement age, I know we will never really retire—we have sons farming. There is always work to be done. I am still the main cook at harvest time. I hope, as we look at ways to pass the farm to our sons, that they have learned that co-operation and teamwork are the keys to a happy farmer.

5. What has your husband's role been?

A very traditional role as "the provider." Although discussions were held, he ultimately made the decisions on major purchases—land, machinery, cattle—as he worked to build a farm to support a family and to encourage the love of farming in his sons.

6. What is the best part for you in this life as a farmwife?

Having three sons farming and raising their children in close proximity to our farm. Watching things grow. I love my weed-free garden and my huge yard. I love to see it all nicely mowed and flowers growing. Growing "food to feed the world" is very satisfying.

7. What is the hardest part?

Realizing my list of "to do" things around the yard has very low priority on my husband and son's list. Things like getting rid of old machinery and tires, or trimming trees.

8. Was feeling isolated ever a part of living on the farm? If so, how did you deal with it?

Yes, but keeping busy was the key! Raising four boys all of whom played hockey, kept you on the road. With church, school (substitute teaching), reading, sewing, knitting, playing cards, visiting friends and neighbours, ski holidays, gardening, mowing grass; there was no time to feel isolated.

9. Were there any "new" traditions that you started in your family?

When I was a kid, our Christmas stockings were old cloth sugar bags. When our kids were little, I made cloth bags out of my grandparents' old curtains. Before my sister Penny died in 2003, she made new cloth bags for my family, which we still use. The adults—now including two daughters-in-law—always get a Christmas stocking bag filled with goodies. (Author's note: I can vouch for this, and they are the best.)

10. Was there anything you were not prepared for prior to becoming a farmwife?

The "drop whatever you're doing and come help me right now" attitude! Also, all the driving required over the years, on the muddy and snow-filled roads, especially in the beginning. Conditions have improved greatly, but I still remember being in the ditch a few times and hitting deer three times.

11. Were there any expectations of you that proved especially difficult?

I filled in at harvest—driving the grain truck and combine—just a few times. I lacked experience and confidence and so it was the worst experience, very hard on the nerves. I was very happy when the kids were "old enough" and I was never called on to do it again.

12. Was there anything that you would have liked to (or that you did) change?

The idea that my kitchen is a restaurant—that the boys can come and go anytime and get fed. Sometimes, I'm pleased that they feel welcome to show up anytime and get fed; other times, I get mad when a meal is ready and they are late or no shows. I am fairly flexible, but quite often I am taken for granted.

13. If there was a legacy that you'd like to leave behind from your life here, what would you like it to be?

I made sure my boys all knew the basics of cooking and some are now excellent cooks (and good at clean-up too!)

Volunteerism—it's important to make time to help your neighbours, community, school, church, sports teams, etc.

Communication and cooperation are key to a successful farm. With three boys farming and sharing equipment, they need to talk, plan and complain less!

14. What is your fall back recipe when you're too tired to plan for supper?

Gary can always survive on canned tomatoes and bread, or a sardine and onion sandwich. For the rest, Denver sandwiches or grilled cheeses. Pancakes work too! Chicken strips, macaroni, tacos all make an easy meal plan, especially when everyone pitches in to help.

15. We've all had unexpected guests pop in; what was a trick that you used to be sure that you were always prepared for company?

Have a well-stocked pantry, baking and garden vegetables in the freezer, and canned fruit and potatoes in the cold room. Now with microwaves meat can be thawed quickly and a meal can usually be ready within the hour.

16. Do you have any words of advice for women who may be marrying a farmer today?

Be yourself. Maintain your interests, but be prepared to put your needs and wants on hold when the farm calls for it. There may not always be funds for an exotic holiday every year: new machinery, land purchases, repair bills take priority. Communication is important—are your goals the same?

17. What is a key piece of advice you would give to help keep a marriage strong?

Remember that nobody is perfect. We all have our selfish moments when we want things to go our way, but it's not always possible! Pick your battles, share your feelings and frustrations, the world won't end if you talk it out. Remember to laugh and enjoy the family and friends you have as you make memories every day. Holidays—together, apart, away from the children, to far away places, or just to the city for a few days—make you appreciate where you live, the lifestyle you enjoy, the friends and family you have, and the marriage you have and want to continue having forever.

18. What is a favourite signature recipe you're willing to share?

SCOTTISH SHORTBREAD

2 cups margarine
1 cup icing sugar
4 scant cups flour

Icing: cold water, colouring, icing sugar.

Mix, rollout, cut with cookie cutters. I use these for Halloween, Christmas, Valentines Day, or any time the grandchildren want to make "rollout" cookies.

My entire reason for doing my first book was so that traditional farmwives everywhere would be recognized, honoured, and held up to their communities. More than that, I wanted **them** to recognize *in themselves* the true gifts that they are—not only to their families, but to Canada's heritage, too.

I feel good knowing that my first book, a true labour of love for me, captured that. I also knew that there was much more to say, and that the next generation needed to have their voices heard too.

About Farmwives 2

When you read the interviews from my first book, you can't help but wonder: "How would today's generation answer the same questions?" I always knew I'd write a second book about the next generations of women referred to, perhaps rather antiquatedly, as "farmwives."

After all, times are changing. My first book honoured the remarkable dedication of traditional farmwives. However, as one of them told me at the time of her interview, "fifty years ago you just did what the person before you did and you didn't think any more about it." Other women told me that there were some things they'd do differently if they'd known better at the time. And one piece of "off the record" advice I will always cherish hearing was "it's only good for the children if it's good for the mom to stay home full-time with them."

Something I learned in my early years as a farmwife was that if I was to absorb all of the duties that could be applied to me, then very quickly I would have no time left to pursue any of my own goals. That's why I decided in those early years that in order to be the best Mom that I could be, it would be imperative for me to design my life in a way that worked for me and my family.

I will be honest and say that I have grown to have an at times conflicted relationship with farming and its lifestyle. Life as a farmwife can involve many different and unique scenarios that don't commonly apply to the marriage-related challenges of the outside world.[1]

---

[1] This is a reeeeeeally good place to mention that *I am not a farm professional, nor am I attempting to offer advice in this section, nor any other section of this book, on that subject.* I am simply a wife/mother/woman who, despite all the love I have for this life, also sees a side to it that I think is spoken about very little. I am pointing out my observations and personal opinions only, and discussing things that have caused *me* concern—and which have required my poor husband to hear me out at length (just ask him ☺).

I wasn't born into the lifestyle of farming. I know that many other "new farmwives" weren't either, and as such I know there had to be others "out there" who had some of the same questions and concerns with the lifestyle that I did. I knew there had to be others that were challenged with "fitting" into traditions that disagreed with their core values; were feeling scared about what would happen if their marriage broke down, or if their husband passed away and they don't have any ownership of their home they've built together and that they worked so hard to care for. What happens if you can't afford to travel to work anymore now that you live on the farm? What happens if your in-laws divorce and you don't have any personal net worth or equity in your family business protecting you from the fall-out? What happens if....? The challenges are endless.

I want women to know that it's okay if they are not fulfilled by spending their days childrearing and tending to a garden. It's okay if you feel resentful if one hundred percent of the housework lands on you in your marriage because it's not typical for farm men to help out. I want you to know that it's okay if you want your role as a farmwife to look different than the one before you.

LIVING ARRANGEMENTS & LAND OWNERSHIP

In some farm families across Canada, it's still common for women to be living in homes they have no ownership over, though they take care of the household entirely. In other scenarios, couples may build homes on land that does not belong to them, but to farm companies. There are many cases in which women spend decades of their marriages living in homes though their name is not on the title and they have no equity in the property. Some women have their names on land owned by their husbands, but many do not. Many dedicate their lives to building a life with their husband with no paperwork or resources in place to protect them should the worst arise.

DIVORCE

It isn't news to anyone that divorce rates are high. I also heard at a succession planning seminar in 2011 that it was not the younger generations who are living out that high statistic, as could be assumed, but the baby boomers that were divorcing more frequently than their younger counterparts.

This caused me to think of the women who decide to divorce amicably after forty plus years with their husbands. They may have no matrimonial property to divide, yet have to start their lives over because the land their house sits on is not owned by them.

DEATH

Farms across Canada are in various stages of succession planning. That is no surprise and that will not change. There are situations where farm husbands have no ownership in family farmland until their predecessors pass away—but what if *they* pass away before that happens? I can't help but wonder about the younger generation wives who risk their security and that of their children if they lose their husband first—do they risk the possibility that they stand to inherit nothing?

Don't get me wrong, I love that marrying a farmer has given me this opportunity to live in a place where my children play in the same yard that their granddad did. I love that my husband used to ride his bike from the house he grew up in to work on the farm with his granddad where we now live. I love that his great grandparents settled this homestead in 1911, and that there are still remnants of them everywhere.

However, countless difficult scenarios still exist for farmwives—those mentioned in this section for a start. It is because of these unique, complicated, and often worrying scenarios that I've included the "Food for Thought" section, which is designed to inspire you to ask your own questions about your farm and set yourself, your family, and your business up in a way that will help you get the very best that farming has to offer—in the twenty-first century.

THE PRESSURE OF A TRADITIONAL LIFESTYLE

I've reflected a lot about the high divorce rates that affect baby boomers in farming, and I couldn't help but think of the women who maybe didn't "love" giving up an opportunity to become something else in their lives.

Those who stayed at home rearing children, while taking on all of the other full-time jobs that a farm entails, and lost themselves in the meantime. Or the women who never heard "thank you" for the endless meals in the field, for stopping whatever she was doing at the drop of a hat, for spending decades taking the chores of "meals and laundry" off the shoulders of the men in her life. What about the women who were underappreciated and uninspired?

Farming is a wonderful and hard life. As great as all of the benefits are, there are very real downsides. I have written this book for one very simple reason: **I do not want families to fail because of the stresses that "traditional farming" puts on "modern families."**

I walked into this life eight years ago with no guidebook; only the guidance of the traditional farmwives all around me, and a feeling in my gut that told me I had to make my life my own.

This book is filled with interviews and stories from more than twenty Canadian women who are doing that very same thing.

I felt a special obligation to write this book especially for the women who weren't able to be a part of it. Like the woman who had to pull out of her interview because in the last year she and her husband are selling their farm and relocating due to a family dispute over an estate, or a woman I had approached who, as much as she wanted to be a part of this second book, declined:

"I had some time to think about the questions you sent, and I'm concerned that if I am honest in answering them (as I would want to be) it could damage relationships here on the farm. I know that could be a whole section of your book that might be helpful, but at this point, I don't want to add any ill feelings out here. The relationship my husband and his father have is fragile, and I've never really "fit in" to farm living as they're used to it, so I worry that being a part of your book will stoke some hostility."

To those women who were able to speak candidly about their farm dynamics, I am so proud of you for digging deep and talking about what are sometimes very personal scenarios and providing "hopeful examples" of ways they have navigated through them.

These scenarios not only still exist; they are going to continue to exist for generations to come. It is all of our responsibilities to help secure the future of farming in Canada by arming ourselves with education, knowledge, and tools that will set our families—and each other—up for success. This book contains stories to inspire you to do just that.

MUSINGS ON A WORD

Let me point out that I fully acknowledge that the term "farmwife"— indeed the entire concept of referring to any woman by what her husband does—is widely considered out-dated. I also fully understand that many women don't feel like a farmwife because they are just as much a farmer as their spouse. In fact, some of the women I approached doing my research chose not to be involved because of their feelings about the word. Fair enough. I can see how the assumption that you are being recognized as someone's wife rather than a woman who farms could seem belittling. And I wish to make myself clear: that is in no way my intention. In fact, even with the seventeen women profiled in my first book being very traditional women, I feel they have been every bit as much a farmer as their husbands.

In this second book, I changed the question "What has the role of farmwife meant to you?" to "What does the term farmwife mean to you, and do you consider yourself to be one?"

As you'll see, the answers to this and the scores of other questions I asked were as varied as the beautiful parts of the country these women hail from. At the end of the day, some women still wear this title like a badge of honour on their sleeve. Others are flat out offended at the term. It is not my place, nor my intent, to "define" any of them. They are very much capable of doing that for themselves.

I am not a sociologist, an anthropologist, or an "expert." Nor do I intend to project my viewpoint on whether or not the term farmwife is right or wrong. I am, instead, going to show you some very different ways that more than twenty amazing Canadian women are living out their very own version of the lifestyle that has typically been described as that of a farmwife.

I decided to forge ahead with using the term farmwife mostly because I gave voice to seventeen women in my first book by honouring them for this very role. It is time now to give that same voice to the newer generations. Whether we consider ourselves "traditional" or "progressive," there are changes happening—important ones. While tradition is still rich throughout this lifestyle and industry, many women are changing how they do things, and changing the expectations others have on them. These new women show how they are demanding more for themselves and their families. No farmwife is better, nor "truer" than any other. That is precisely the point. I simply want to know how the idea of the farmwife is changing. I know it is. We all know that it is. This book will show us how.

INTERVIEWS: The New Canadian Farmwives

INTERVIEW #1: Cherilyn Jolly-Nagel

(*Photo Credit: Sandra Jennett of Silver Blue Photography*)

Age at this writing: 37

I heard Cherilyn Jolly-Nagel speak at a "Celebrating Women in Farming" Event in Saskatoon, Saskatchewan in November 2016. I was instantly taken by her infectious passion for farming, her vast knowledge of the industry, her professionalism, wit and humour. I knew she would provide a great interview for this second book.

Cherilyn and her husband David's farm name is Hunter's Paradise Farming and Outfitting and is located northwest of Mossbank, Saskatchewan. They work as a team with his brother Mike and wife Natalie. They, along with their other full-time employees, grow durum, canola, chickpeas and lentils.

Here's what she said when I asked her:

Q: What does the term 'farmwife' mean to you, and do you consider yourself to be one?

A: "I have always struggled with the term "farmwife." Not because I don't have a deep appreciation for the women in my ancestry and in my life who proudly filled that role but because I never identified with it. I recall filling out those annoying forms that ask for your name, date of birth, and of course "Occupation". I asked myself the question, Is "farmers wife" an occupation? Or could I be so bold as to say I was a farmer too? So I tested it out. I rebelliously wrote Farmer in the blank line beside Occupation. Nothing bad happened. So I did it again and again. Eventually I said it out loud and with more conviction. I am a farmer. I pass no judgment towards women who call themselves farmwives, in fact I'm a bit jealous that they are comfortable with it. But for me, in order to own this crazy decision to move home and find a place in this industry, calling myself a farmer was the first step."

Q: What was your background prior to marrying your husband?

A: "Even though I come from generations of farmers, I never envisioned a future for myself on the farm. In fact, if there was one thing I knew for sure when I graduated high school... it was that I was NOT going to be a farmer. I was interested in travelling the world and took a diploma program in Hospitality and Tourism Marketing. I chose a myriad of experiences including being a Latin dance instructor on the beaches of the Turks and Caicos Islands."

Q: Briefly describe your family farm business and it's key players. If you have a business or career "off the farm"? Tell me about that, too.

A: " Our farm name is *Hunter's Paradise Farming and Outfitting* and David and I work as a team with his brother Mike and wife Natalie. We employ many other people full time and throughout the growing season. We grow durum, canola, chickpeas and lentils.

I have found a special interest in agricultural policy work and have been volunteering with the Western Canadian Wheat Growers Association and other boards for more than 15 years. I was the associations youngest and first female President and I continue to dedicate my time to the board as a Director.

I am also working with Farm and Food Care as a facilitator for "the Real Dirt on Farming" training program that encourages other farmers and ranchers to speak up about our modern agricultural practices with the goal of answering the questions consumers have about food and farming. I thoroughly enjoy taking the stage and speaking to a wide array of audiences about my amazing life in agriculture.

I sit on a number of other boards that aim to promote positive changes to the business of agriculture, including the Agriculture Development Fund through the Sask Ministry of Ag, I Chair the Sask Agri-Value Initiative (SAVI) and I have recently been invited to sit as an International Director with the Global Farmer Network.

Q: What do you consider your primary role?

A: "I guess that depends on what season it is and what hat I'm wearing that day. The best part of our business is that my day never looks the same. While the girls are still at home, my primary role is to be their mom and support the farm wherever I'm needed. I take on some of the farm administrative duties and spend countless hours building and maintaining the necessary relationships."

Q: Do you ever feel that being a "farmwife" takes away from any other personal goals you may have?

A: "If I'm being honest, then yes there were times after I moved home to start this life on the farm that I did feel my own personal goals would be sacrificed in order to support my husbands lifestyle/career. At that time, I took little to no ownership (neither tangible nor heartfelt) in the farm operation. Even after thoroughly enjoying my time taking an Agriculture Diploma from Olds College, I still didn't really believe that I could be happy as a farmer. But I was good at faking it. It wasn't until I discovered the world of farm policy that I began to settle in and get comfortable. It took years of being an advocate and a fighter for positive changes in the industry before I looked back and realized that I had found my place.

Q: On some Canadian farms where multiple families are involved, there are a variety of land and home-ownership complexities that still exist today. In terms of the ownership setup of your farm – is there anything that worries you about your own or your children's security?

A: "The structure of our farm in terms of profit share and ownership has changed many times since David and I moved home to farm with his parents. It is constantly evolving and adapting. With the help of our accounting team we've gone from operating as several sole proprietors to incorporating as one economic unit. It is much more efficient and consolidated. When David's parents moved into a retirement position, a succession plan was put in place and is being carried out over a number of years. Now we each have young families and we are all working together to ensure the viability of our farm. Provided our lines of communication stay open, I don't see any need to worry.

Q: Has there been anything you were not prepared for since becoming a "farmwife"?

A: "Nope it all went exactly as I knew it would. NOT! I had no grand illusions that life on the farm would be easy but I did not predict how much the farm would dictate our everyday. I'm not envious of my friends who work a 9-5 job but I suppose the predictability of income and of "Time off" would've been nice at times. We do our best to make time for the kids and travel with them but we really haven't figured out how to leave the work that needs to be done. On a positive note, I also wasn't prepared for how much I would come to love the land and all the beauty and grit that comes with it.

Q: What do you think is a key lesson we can learn from the older generation of farmwives – and also, what is a great piece of advice you've been given from the older generation that you've valued?

A: "I have tremendous respect for the farm women who have come before me. At 91 my grandma continues to inspire me by keeping up with the goings on of her large family. She once told me that the thing she misses the most from living on the farm is the smell of dirt. Every year she comes out to help me plant a garden. My mom stayed at home with my siblings and me and she supported my dad in more ways than were ever recognized. From gourmet lunches and meals in the field to sewing dance costumes and running her own business, my mom made everything look easy! As a mother now, I'm so grateful for all that she did for us and all that I took for granted. It's because of her that regardless of my career aspirations, being here for my kids is the most important job I have. I've also been blessed with a kind and caring mother-in-law. She has always made me feel part of this farm and part of this family.

Q: What is a hilarious story you can share about life on your farm?

A: "I can laugh at many situations I've found myself in over the years! Possibly the one David and I giggle about the most was when I got stuck underneath the air drill! It was late one night and I was helping fill the drill with seed and fertilizer and even at 8 months pregnant I didn't give it a second thought to crawling on the ground to check the air flow and ensure no boots were plugged. Working my way from one end to the other with my baby belly dragging on the ground, I got right near the middle of the 50 ft. drill and realized this task was not as easy I remembered it to be. I called out to David that I was **stuck**! He, in his usual helpful and empathetic manner, laughed out loud and offered little in the way of advice. I did eventually "back it up" and find an exit but was exhausted from the effort! Only when I could stretch out on the ground did I join David in laughter. Claire (the baby along for the ride) was destined for a life of *tagging along* with her mom!

Q: Do you have an "app" or "hack" to keep yourself organized that you cannot live without?

A: "Yes, I have a secret app that I call "relying on other people!" It's invaluable! There are so many people in my life that help me to get through the hectic weeks that come and go. Our parents are often called upon to help with the kids schedules and I have friends that go out of their way to support me when I'm at meetings. I have reminder alerts set on my phone that keep away the "oh shit I'm supposed to be somewhere" moments. The whiteboard calendars on the fridge in the kitchen keep our family running together in the right direction. David and I touch base many times throughout the day and that ensures that we get done what needs to be done.

Q: What do you consider the biggest challenge for "women" entering or living life on the farm?

A: "Finding my place on the farm was the certainly the biggest challenge. I never wanted to be a farmer so I didn't have a vision of what this life looked like with me in it. I tried all kinds of jobs related to agriculture like loading railcars, scouting fields, farm accounting, and operating equipment. All of those tasks combined gave me a sense of what the industry was about. David was born to be a farmer. I had to learn to love it. Once I quit fighting the feeling that coming back to my hometown to farm was a letdown, I began to appreciate the amazing life I was being offered. There's no place I'd rather be and no better way to raise children.

Q: What are ways you try to keep your marriage strong?

A: "I'm not a romantic person. I don't believe in love at first sight and I don't believe that there is only one right person in this world for everyone. Marriage is built on trust, fun, and an understanding of who you are alone—and together. It might sound strange but keeping our marriage strong has had less to do with my relationship with David and more to do with the relationship I have with myself. Looking back, the times when our marriage was difficult was often when I struggled with my own purpose. The happier I've become with who I am and what I love to do, the happier our marriage is. David has never tried to influence what I do next; he simply supports me and insists that I value my time and efforts. If it weren't for him, I'd do everything for free! Mutual respect and admiration make us an amazing team, in our parenting, in our farm business and in our marriage. And after 21 years I still get butterflies in my stomach when he comes home.

Q: For grain farmers – "harvest" is undoubtedly the busiest time of the year. How are harvest meals are managed on your farm? (If you're not a grain farmer – pick an equally busy time of year on your farm and describe how meal-times are managed)

A: "When I first moved to the farm and started cooking meals for the crew I followed the Nagel tradition of taking out TWO hot meals every-day! It was exhausting and after having our first baby it was unrealistic! Years later, we are much more efficient. The kitchen in the shop is stocked with lunch items for the crew to pack when they come to punch in for the day. My sister in law and I take turns cooking the supper meal. Both Natalie and I have spent time operating the equipment in the field and we know how valuable the supper meal is to a working crew. We cook and deliver the best meals we can and I think we both have fun doing it. Sharing the job allows us time to spend with our kids and plan for the week. Natalie is wonderful to work with because of her organizational skills. We text each other to switch meal days and do what is needed to support each other when parenting or work obligations fall into the busy season.

Q: What is something you do for self-care when farm life, family life and work are so time-consuming?

A: "I do best under pressure, in fact complacency makes me uncomfortable. So I don't require a lot during the busy seasons, I'm actually happier working than when I'm supposed to have down time. Exercise is the one thing that I do truly require for mental clarity. If my days in the office or in meetings are so full that I don't get time to move I can start to feel sluggish. I mix up the workouts so I never get bored. I also recommend that women take holidays alone. Yes, alone. Just a few days completely by myself forces me to take care of me. It's a cool experience to take time away from everyone and just be with myself.

Q: Having our families eat nutritious meals is becoming more and more a priority to families. Spending less "time" in the kitchen to achieve that, however, is also a necessity. What is a GREAT recipe your family can share that achieves both of these goals?

HOT SAUCE SALMON

Place large filet of salmon on tin foil and cover with
Lemon juice
Pepper
Fresh dill
Garlic
Franks RedHot
Catalina Dressing

Wrap in several layers of tinfoil

BBQ for 12 minutes and flip over for another 12 minutes.

Add sauce mixture of more hotsauce and Catalina dressing before serving. Serve with green beans fried with dill and lemon. The harvest crew loves this easy, nutritious meal and a bonus for me is that I can buy GMO Salmon! This makes me very happy!

Age at this writing: 40

I was introduced to Kathryn by Lynn Prevost of the Association of Canadian Custom Harvesters Inc., at a conference in 2016. Kathryn Doyle and her husband are custom harvesters who live south of Fort Macleod, Alberta. They›ve been married nearly nineteen years. The introduction started with "Kathryn has *SIX* kids!" Knowing custom harvesting requires months of travel, I knew I had to find out how she did it!

Kathryn and her husband Ryan start combining in Oklahoma and finish in Alberta, all with their children and about ten employees in tow. What convinced me that Kathryn had to be in my book wasn't just that she looked far too "put together" and calm to be the mother of six children, but the look in her eyes when she answered my first question, "How do you do it?"

She looked at me with a warm smile and said, "I just love being a mom."

Kathryn is warm, humble, extremely dedicated to her family business, and the perfect example for those who say 'there are no traditional farm women left.'"

Q: What does the term 'farmwife' mean to you, and do you consider yourself to be one?

A: "To me, being a farmwife is supporting my husband. To be able to be a wife, a mom, and a farmer."

Q: Briefly describe your family farm business and its key players. If you have a business or career "off the farm," tell me about that, too.

A: " We both have always wanted to farm. The prices often are high, so we stayed in agriculture by custom harvesting. We both grew up on farms and are still hoping to farm in the future. We start combining in Oklahoma and finish in Alberta."

Q: What do you consider your primary role?

A: "My primary role is keeping everyone happy. We have up to twelve employees and six kids. I feed them all and do laundry and run combine."

Q: What is the best part of life on a farm for you?

A: "The lifestyle, for us and for our kids. It teaches amazing work ethic and we ALL work together.

Q: On some Canadian farms where multiple families are involved, there are a variety of land- and home-ownership complexities that still exist today. In terms of the ownership setup of your farm, is there anything that worries you about your own or your children's security?

A: "Ryan and I purchased a place right between both our parents' homes where we grew up. My mom and dad's parents are two miles east of us. My parents sold the home quarter about nine years ago. Right after that my mom got sick with inflammatory breast cancer. We lost her in March 2009. I miss her terribly. She was such a good and faithful servant, full of faith, and she loved us kids and Dad so much! My dad has since remarried my mom's best friend. Her husband died before my mom and he was my dad's very good friend. She treats us all very well and loves us just like she always had when we were younger. I have a great deal of respect for her and love her too. She has eleven boys and two girls. So, her and Dad have twenty kids and numerous in-laws and grandkids.

Ryan's parents still live out here on the same gravel road as us. Ryan and his dad to a lot together and share the shop. We are just in the process of selling our place to move back to Ryan's homeplace. Most places have a name so I refer to this as the 'Klorn Place' because the Klorns homesteaded it. There are two houses on this place; my in-laws live in one, which was moved on by my father in-law with his semi. We hope to move into it, as it's twice as big as the house we are currently in—which is 1,100 square feet with eight of us. The other house on the Klorn Place is empty and needs to be cleaned up. We'd put up a new house for my in-laws, which would be beneficial to us and to them. We could be close to the shop and all our work, and we are young enough and have enough energy to fix up the house they are in. In turn, they would have a new house and a family to help them. We have always considered family very important and we hope that my mom-in-law and father in-law could stay there longer if we were around. My mom-in-law has diabetes and it would be nice to be able to just run over to her house rather than drive if she doesn't answer the phone (which happens). We need to be close to get sugar in her quickly, and we could do the yard work and help in other ways as well.

I think this is one of the best things about good values and showing love … looking after your parents, helping each other out to make the road smoother. Both sets of our parents have been incredibly helpful to both Ryan and I, and of course they raised us! This transition seems like it should be black and white, but it's not because there is so much to consider. Who's name should be on the title? Who will live in the new house if and when Ryan's parents make a change? We have six kids—will they all want to, or none? Is it smart to build a new house for a couple who may want to move to town soon? Should they just live here (our house is completely done—I love that kind of work so every year I've done a project on this house) … These are all challenges and decisions we are trying to mull through. Making decisions with love and wisdom is sometimes a tedious job."

Q: What is a hilarious story you can share about life on your farm?

A: "My daughter to our laying hens: 'Do not worry hen pennies, your friends are in the freezer in the shop, we just plucked them.'

Q: Do you have an app or "hack" to keep yourself organized that you cannot live without?

A: "I am very organized with a big family and large crew to feed so that is my 'hack'! I'm not technical at all. I start my day the same every day and follow routine, for example: windows every Tuesday, mending Wednesday, lunches made and packed by 7 am every day, laundry done by 10 am, supper going well before men come in for lunch. I have two lives: one at home and one for four months on the road."

Q: What are some ways you try to keep your marriage strong?

A: "We do parts runs together when we can! Fieldwork together. We mostly just work as a team. I could not do this without him or our kids."

Q: For grain farmers, harvest is undoubtedly the busiest time of the year. How are harvest meals managed on your farm? (If you're not a grain farmer, pick an equally busy time of year on your farm and describe how meal times are managed.)

A: "On the road is our busiest time ... we harvest wheat, oats, barley, canola, and pulse crops from Oklahoma to Alberta.

My morning typically begins at 6 am. I get food prepared for my six kids and about ten hired men. Once breakfast is done, the girls and I dress the boys and start laundry for about eighteen people. We take turns on dishes and laundry and taking care of the three little boys. Liam runs combine and goes with Ryan to the field. I start supper right after breakfast, preparing salads, peeling potatoes, and starting meat. I then do a grocery run and call Ryan to see if he may need anything.

When I come back to the trailer we try to find spots for all the food that feeds the eighteen of us. I like things neat and tidy so this is challenging in our trailer house on wheels. Then I feed the kids lunch and start baking for lunches for the next day and prepare dessert. Once that is done, I finish up supper and pack up the suburban with food, chairs, tables, and kids. We eat in the field and then we head back. I bath the boys in a Rubbermaid container and Kierstyn and Grace do the many dishes (no paper for me). Once the three little boys are in bed, the girls and I pack the men's lunches for the next day and set out baking and hot coffee for when they come in. A quick clean of our Miss Hilton (trailer) and we are done for the day, usually at 10 p m.

At home ... just add sports, 4H, yard upkeep, and visits!

Q: Having our families eat nutritious meals is becoming more and more a priority to families. Spending less time in the kitchen to achieve that, however, is also a necessity. What is a GREAT recipe your family can share that achieves both of these goals?

A: "I'm pretty old school. I still can and freeze all of my veggies in the fall. I put away about six hundred quarts. I can beans, carrots, corn, beets, jam, pickles, spaghetti sauce. I freeze my peas. We raise our own beef and chickens and get hogs from a local colony—that's where I get all my fresh produce to can, as well. I start canning in Montana and finish at home. I also grind my own wheat, which Liam (our oldest) grows and cleans for me."

Auntie Evelyns Buns ④

2 3/4 cups warm water
1/2 tbsp salt
1 1/2 tbsp suger
1/4 cup oil
1 egg
3-3 1/2 cups whole wheat
  mix
1 heaping tbsp yeast
4-6 cup white flour
Knead for 10 min

Warm a little oil in large tupperware in warm
oven. oil hands. form dough into ball

⑤

and let rise for 20 min covered in warm
oven. punch down and rise 10 min. (get next
things ready.
-plate w warm oil, line pans w parchment paper.
form buns with oil, approx 20 buns per sheet.

Let rise in warm oven with light on for 1 hr.
  Bake @ 375 20 min.

INTERVIEW #3: Amanda Hammond O'Connell

Age at this writing: 35

Amanda Hammond O'Connell is from Carleton Place, Ontario. Amanda and her husband of eight years have taken over her family's farm. They have two daughters, Margaret (five) and Mackenzie (two).

Q: What does the term 'farmwife' mean to you, and do you consider yourself to be one?

A: "This is hard question! Farmwife is a plethora of things to me. It's a wife and mom, a cook, a bookkeeper, etc. Essentially, a farmwife is a woman who does countless jobs with little to no recognition, but is an essential part of keeping the farm running and successful. And no, I don't think of myself as just a farmwife. I am a farmer, a wife, and a mom."

Q: What was your background prior to marrying your husband?

A: "I was raised on a dairy cash crop farm. We started with a small tie stall barn and lost the barn and eighty animals in a barn fire in 1992. My family rebuilt a free stall barn, and we are still milking in it today. My father married my mom: a city girl who always said she was "married to a farmer, *not* a farmer's wife," so I grew up with the best of both worlds—we lived on the farm and had everything that came with it, but we also spent time travelling and were involved in a lot of things we wouldn't have had the opportunity to experience if my mother was on the farm like I am today.

My husband and I met when we were both attending college and studying agriculture. I went on to the University of Guelph, where I received my Bachelor of Science Degree in Agriculture with Honours. Over the years I have worked in pest and disease management. Once, returning home from school, I worked for a seed company doing research and market development. My husband and I had been dating just eight months when we decided we would like to farm. This is when we started the succession process to take over the 50 percent share of my family's farm from my grandfather. We farmed for almost two years before getting married."

Q: Briefly describe your family farm business and its key players. If you have a business or career "off the farm," tell me about that, too.

A: "Sunol Farms Ltd. is now a third-generation dairy farm in my family. We milk 110 Holstein cows. We replaced our parlour with Lely robots just two years ago. We also crop about 2,500 acres growing corn, soybeans, wheat, and hay. My father is a 50-percent-partner with my husband and myself and works from April to November, then winters in Florida. I was offered a Dow Seeds dealership when I left the company, and I sell seed to other farms in the area. My husband sells hay and straw throughout the year as well."

Q: What do you consider your primary role?

A: "On the farm side, the day to day operations—I take care of the cows and calves, breed, oversee crop management, and do all book work and accounting. On the home side, I take care of the girls, giving them the tools to grow up and be people I can be proud of."

Q: Have you started any new traditions in your family that are important to you?

A: "Every second year my husband and I take an adults-only trip. It rejuvenates us, and our relationship. With so much emphasis put on the farm and the business, I think it's important to work on us sometimes. Also, on the weekends its "all hands on deck" and the girls come and help feed calves, sweep the barn, and wash robot the rooms with us."

Q: On some Canadian farms where multiple families are involved, there are a variety of land- and home-ownership complexities that still exist today. In terms of the ownership setup of your farm, is there anything that worries you about your own or your children's security?

A: "In the past, definitely. My grandfather was the primary landowner of all the property we farmed, including the barns, sheds, and two houses. He had said he was willing them to my father, but we really had no way of knowing. In the end, the land went to my father and the crisis was averted. This, however, was an eye-opener to my father and myself. All the land and buildings are now co-owned by my father and me. Wills have all been updated to protect my parents, my husband, and my children if the worst-case scenario were ever to occur. We have also committed to updating wills and any other business agreements every five years."

Q: What do you think is a key lesson we can learn from the older generation of farmwives, and what is a great piece of advice you've been given from the older generation that you've valued?

A: "I think the biggest take-home message from the farmwives in my life is: Do what makes you happy, end of story. If you enjoy making meals and taking care of the kids, do that. If you like putting in the crop and working on machinery, do that. If you like milking cows, do that. If you like working in town and are not involved in the day-to-day operations, do that. The greatest advice, besides doing what makes you happy, is to ignore the people who try to put you down. Their negativity usually has less to do with what you are doing and more what they are not doing. And finally, prove them wrong."

Q: What is a hilarious story you can share about life on your farm?

A: "My husband is from a beef farm, and was a cattle drover before we took over the dairy, so there was a steep learning curve. When I have laughed the most is when I was teaching him the ways of dairy farming.

Teaching him how to milk in the parlour and cows pooping on his head, then him jumping back and another cow peeing on his head ... All super funny until it happens to you.

We had a really big cow having a hard calving and the calf needed to be pulled. My husband wanted to do it. I said "Okay, put on the gloves."

"I have gloves on."

"No ... the really long gloves,"

A look of terror crossed his face.

Once the gloves were on, he stuck his hand up the cow's back end, and I told him to feel around to figure out what he was feeling. After a little while he screamed and threw is hand out of the cow.

"That calf just bit me!!!"

I was literally on the ground laughing.

Another one of my funny moments came when I was walking the cornfields looking for armyworm. I was in the middle of a hundred-acre field and I really had to go to the bathroom. As any farm girl knows, you always carry toilet paper with you. So I popped a squat and peed ... well, when I went to stand up there was a very large buck about two feet from my face. I screamed and turned around to run, but my pants were around my ankles and I dove head first into the ground. Thankfully the deer had the same idea and ran the other way."

Q: What do you consider the biggest challenge for women entering into / living life on the farm?

A: "The biggest is the fact that we have to prove ourselves more so then the men in our industry. I am just not strong enough to lift a 1,200 pound cow. You are considered beneath a man in the same position until you prove them wrong, and in some cases you will never change their perception of you. But for me, I never really cared, because the fact is that it is the *perception*, or a prejudgment they have of you, not what or who you really are. At the end of the day, do your job, kick ass, and people (men and women) will respect that."

Q: For grain farmers, harvest is undoubtedly the busiest time of the year. How are harvest meals managed on your farm? (If you're not a grain farmer, pick an equally busy time of year on your farm and describe how meal times are managed.)

A: "I always have the best of intentions, I swear! I love my Crock-pot, and will try and throw stuff into it in the morning, but a lot of the time it's sandwiches, and sometimes a run to town for takeout (if I haven't been to the grocery store in two weeks). Other times, I rely on our mums. My mother and my mother-in-law will stop what they are doing and whip up some food and drive it out to the field for us. We would probably starve without them."

Q: As you know, the demands of farming on your spouse's time is often such that they cannot contribute as much to home or childcare as spouses who work forty hours a week can. Describe how the never-ending task of housework is managed in your home.

A: "This is definitely a bone of contention with my husband and I, as I work just as many hours on the farm. I do all of the housework and somehow make it work: laundry in the middle of the night, cleaning before breakfast … it never gets done all at once, it's more a continuous cycle. As for the kids, as they say, "it takes a village!" Our oldest is in school now, and our youngest goes to a sitter most of the week, so that is a huge help during the "normal" workday hours, but before and after that we shuffle them around a lot. Most of the time they are with me; sometimes one will go to the field in the tractor with Daddy or Poppa. On top of that we have our mums—we would be lost without them. They take the girls whenever they can, sometimes for sleepovers during planting and harvest when we are out all night."

Q: Having our families eat nutritious meals is becoming more and more a priority for families. Spending less time in the kitchen to achieve that, however, is also a necessity. What is a GREAT recipe your family can share that achieves both of these goals?

SLOW-COOKER CHICKEN CHILI

2 x 28 oz. cans of diced tomatoes
1 x 28 oz. can of crushed tomatoes
2–3 15 oz. cans of beans or lentils (whatever you have)
2 x 15 oz. cans of corn
1 box / 4 cups of chicken broth
4–6 chicken breasts, cut into cubes
1 tbsp. garlic powder or a couple of cloves, diced
1 tbsp. onion powder or 1/2 an onion, chopped
1 tsp. pepper flakes
6 tsp. chili powder
1–2 cups quinoa

Pop everything into the Crock-pot, stir, and cook for 6–8 hours on low or 4–6 hours on high. Pile with cheese, sour cream, onions, guacamole, tortilla chips, or garlic bread. The best thing about this recipe is that you can substitute whatever you want; mine has never tasted the same twice. ;)

INTERVIEW #4: Nicolle Downey

Age at this writing: 30

Nicolle Downey hails from Tarantum, Prince Edward Island (twenty minutes east of Charlottetown). She's lived there for eight years. She has been married to her husband for four-and-a-half, and they have three children. When she saw one of my "call outs" on social media for the "new generation" of farm women, she contacted me and was eager to answer my questions.

Q: "What does the term 'farmwife' mean to you, and do you consider yourself to be one?

A: "Farmwife ... to me it means not only being the wife of a farmer, but also a mom, a chef, a gopher for farm parts, a chauffeur, a shoulder to cry on, an ear to listen about the day's work and what was accomplished. Also a friend to laugh with."

Q: Briefly describe your family farm business and its key players. If you have a business or career "off the farm," tell me about that, too.

A: "We have been growing cereal crops and soy beans for about ten years, and most recently two years ago we purchased a twenty-head beef herd."

Q: What do you consider your primary role?

A: "My primary role is to care for our children, my husband, and our house."

Q: What is your husband's role in your family and on the farm?

A: "My husband is basically a one-man show. He does everything he can himself, otherwise we hire for some seasonal work to help with planting and harvesting our crop. My husband cares for our cattle twice daily, fixes machinery, prepares and harvests our crop. He also does the business part of the farm, buying and selling equipment, crop, straw, and hay."

Q: Do you ever feel that being a farmwife takes away from any other personal goals you may have?

A: "It can be a very demanding job. So yes, it does take away from some goals or other things I am interested in doing."

Q: What is a hilarious story you can share about life on your farm?

A: "The time my husband asked me to tow him home in the tractor with his big dually truck. He told me not to go past third gear, but when I looked back in my mirror he was holding his hand up and moving it. I assumed that meant fifth gear, so I sped up into fifth gear and he was holding on for dear life in the tractor as I towed him going about 100 kilometres per hour. He was in fact telling me to stop or slow down! To this day I still can't tell the story without laughing. Not to mention it was fall and the neighbours were out in the potato field harvesting potatoes and thinking, 'What the heck is going on?? They must be in a hurry!'"

Q: For grain farmers, harvest is undoubtedly the busiest time of the year. How are harvest meals managed on your farm? (If you're not a grain farmer, pick an equally busy time of year on your farm and describe how meal times are managed.)

A: "My husband has fields close to home and others that aren't so close to home. When he is nearby he eats breakfast before heading to the field and usually skips lunch. Then I take a hot supper to the field for him and usually a couple workers."

Q: Having our families eat nutritious meals is becoming more and more a priority for families. Spending less time in the kitchen to achieve that, however, is also a necessity. What is a GREAT recipe your family can share that achieves both of these goals?

A: "Some days it takes all day for me to meal prep. I try to get it done while the baby is napping. I also prep casseroles and freeze them for days where it isn't possible for healthy meals to be made. We are a big 'meat and veggies' family, but when we need a change, this Taco Bake is easy and delicious."

TACO BAKE

1 cup cooked brown rice
1 lb. lean turkey or beef
1/2 cup pepper, chopped
1/4 cup onion, chopped
Taco seasoning (I use Epicure)
2 x 8 oz. cans of tomato sauce
4 cups shredded cheese

Directions: Cook beef with taco seasoning. Add veggies and tomato sauce, bring to a boil, and simmer for a few minutes. Add cooked rice and two cups of cheese. Mix in a pan, add remaining cheese over top and bake in oven for twenty minutes.

INTERVIEW #5: Tiffany Martinka

(*Photo Credit: Damara Lynn Photography*)

Age at this writing: 31

Tiffany hails from St. Benedict, Saskatchewan. She's lived there for eight years now. She's been married to her husband for eight years and they have three children.

Q: What does the term 'farmwife' mean to you, and do you consider yourself to be one?

A: "Meeting many farm families over the years, the term farmwife means so much more to me than ever before. To me, she is the one quietly behind the scenes, ensuring everything is operating smoothly. She is primary caregiver for the children, she is ensuring the fridge is stocked and complete meals are on the table—which isn't an easy task when for some farm women the closest grocery store is a half an hour or more away. Many times it is the farmwife that completes all the book work for the farm and ensures all documentation needed for the farm season is up to date.

Farmwives are the support that the farm needs in order to successfully operate. They are chameleons that transform to fit whatever role the farm needs that day. While I do consider myself a farmwife, I don't think that is the only title that I place on myself. We all have many labels; mine include "Brandt's mom," "runner," "territory manager." I think it is also important to note that many farmwives would also be considered a farmer. Each one of us manages this role differently, in a way that works for us, our families, and our farms. I am proud to be a farmwife and to support our farm to the best of my ability."

Q: What was your background prior to marrying your husband?

A:"I grew up the oldest of five children on a mixed grain-and-cattle farm. It was very important that we helped out around the farm and were involved in many aspects. From there, I did a farm stay in New Zealand for eight months, prior to attending university. I attended the College of Agriculture at the University of Saskatchewan and was heavily involved in many extracurricular and student councils. I also worked in agriculture retail during my summers in university."

Q: Briefly describe your family farm business and its key players. If you have a business or career "off the farm," tell me about that, too.

A: "Our family farm involves multiple families. Originally it was three brothers (my husband's father and two uncles) who started Martinka Dairy. As time progressed, they either had to completely upgrade the dairy or get out. They chose to get out of dairy and instead invest in a broiler chick operation. When it came time for my husband to farm full time, we began the process of buying out my father-in-law's third of the corporation. So, currently we farm with two uncles. Our farm places 100,000 chicks each cycle and we also farm 2,000 acres of grain land. I also have a full-time career in the agriculture industry. I have spent a few years as an extension agronomist and am now currently in a sales role, working closely with producers and Ag retail. I also believe strongly in agriculture advocacy. I have been working on building my blog, www.prairiepretty.com where you can follow our farm story."

Q: What is the best part of life on a farm for you?

A: "Harvest! It is my absolute favourite and I feel it brings us closer together as a family. My boys love spending every minute they can on the combine or grain cart with their dad, grandpa, uncles, or cousins. The food seems to taste better when we eat meals in the field. And there is a feeling of excitement and pride as you harvest what everyone worked so hard for all year long. The stress of weather and pest management is finally over, and the commodity is safely in the bin."

Q: Have you started any new traditions in your family that are important to you?

A: "No electronics or TV at the supper table!"

Q: On some Canadian farms where multiple families are involved, there are a variety of land- and home-ownership complexities that still exist today. In terms of the ownership setup of your farm, is there anything that worries you about your own or your children's security?

A: "We have multiple families involved and we made sure the right conditions for everyone were in place before we moved onto the home farm and invested money into renovating the farmhouse. My advice would be to work with professionals to ensure the right agreements are in place. It can be very complex and very confusing. Reach out for help!

I think this is super-important to do *before* you make any transitions. When family is involved, you want to make sure everything is handled properly so that no assumptions are made and no hard feelings come about. Everything needs to be clear and concise."

Q: Has there been anything you were not prepared for since becoming a farmwife?

A: "I grew up on a farm so I knew that farming often meant long hours with my dad away and that the farm was often priority. Now that I am a farmwife and raising my own family, I understand that the farm is priority for my husband, and that it means the same long hours at work. However, when you have children and are managing the household and everything else, those hours seem SO much longer than I remember. Everything is magnified and intensified when you go from being the daughter of a farmer to the wife of a farmer. I often joke that I am a seasonal single mom: during seeding and harvest."

Q: What do you think is a key lesson we can learn from the older generation of farmwives, and what is a great piece of advice you've been given from the older generation that you've valued?

A: "When I think about the older generation, I am always amazed at how giving and selfless they all were! They were key components to the farms' success, and the cornerstones to many communities, schools, and churches, working hard to build them up to what they are today. So much of their time and their entire lives were invested in the farm and the communities, and never did they expect to receive recognition. It was just what they did and what they believed in. They were true leaders."

Q: What is a hilarious story you can share about life on your farm?

A: "My oldest son lives for getting to do cattle chores with his grandpa. We were once visiting when he was around two or three years old. I think he was getting ready for a bath when he realized his grandpa had gone outside and he thought he was missing out on chores. Well, he made a beeline for the door and ran outside wearing nothing but his rubber boots! All we could see was his little bare butt in the middle of the yard yelling for Grandpa! He was determined that he was not going to miss doing those chores."

Q: Do you have an app or "hack" to keep yourself organized that you cannot live without?

A: "We keep a calendar front-and-centre in the kitchen. Everything gets written down. If my husband comes to tell me about something he has going on, my response is "Write it on the calendar!" We refer to it daily."

Q: Is there any piece of advice you wish you had received when beginning your life as a farmwife, and what advice would you give to women marrying into farm life today?

A: "The farm itself can be a full-time job! I'm not talking about the actual farming—I'm talking about the upkeep of the farm. Cutting the grass in summer takes hours, snow removal in the winter the same. It takes longer for any type of maintenance workers to come to your home, the driving for children's activities or groceries will be a much longer commute, and it takes a lot of time and planning to make it happen! Invest in a big slow-cooker and a good vehicle!"

Q: For grain farmers, harvest is undoubtedly the busiest time of the year. How are harvest meals managed on your farm? (If you're not a grain farmer, pick an equally busy time of year on your farm and describe how meal times are managed.)

A: "On our farm, the men are responsible for their own breakfast and packing their own lunch, as well as any snacks or drinks that are needed for the day. The farmwives bring out supper. There are three families involved, so we share the workload. Each woman takes on three meals in a row, then we rotate like that until harvest is complete. This way, if it rains or there's a breakdown, etc., we all know we still need to get in our three meals until supper duty is handed off to the next person."

Q: When it all just seems too much (life, responsibilities, the juggling act) what is something you do for self-care?

A: "I try to remind myself that something as simple as washing my face at the end of the day and taking the time to put lotion on my body before bed can be considered self-care. But when I have the motivation I love to go for a run. Living rural, it is super easy to step out the door and be back in a half hour from a nice run. The fresh air and scenery is refreshing!"

Q: Having our families eat nutritious meals is becoming more and more a priority for families. Spending less time in the kitchen to achieve that, however, is also a necessity. What is a GREAT recipe your family can share that achieves both of these goals?

A: "Cookie Balls! (They're also called "Energy Bites" but we call them Cookie Balls because to us, they taste just like cookies—and then the boys also think they are getting a treat!) They are super easy to grab on the go, and wholesome enough to give for breakfast if needed."

COOKIE BALLS

1 cup rolled oats
1/3 ground flax (grabbed my flax straight from the bin!)
1 tbsp. vanilla
1/3 cup chocolate chips
1/2 cup peanut butter
1/3 cup honey

Mix together with hands and roll into balls.

INTERVIEW #6: Melanie Jespersen

(*Photo: supplied*)

Age at this writing: 41

This next interview is of someone I admire greatly. She's been in my life for forty-one years and she's not only my cousin but an amazing, lifelong friend. We have been through a lot, and despite very different upbringings, we have both serendipitously found ourselves married to farmers. Melanie and her husband live on MBJ Farms Ltd. just south of Taber, Southern Alberta, with their two children.

Q: What does the term 'farmwife' mean to you, and do you consider yourself to be one?

A: "So many points come to mind when I hear "farmwife." Not only does it include the stereotypical jobs around the house and yard, it involves so much more. My husband is so knowledgeable when it comes to the farm operations and he is continually advancing the farm by researching new concepts, applications, etc. I feel my role complements Marty's strengths, and I can add a different perspective at times. I feel it is a partnership, with both of us playing important roles for the overall success of the business. I absolutely feel I am a farmwife; I devote 100 percent of my time and energy to my family and the farm."

Q: What was your background prior to marrying your husband?

A: "I grew up on a acreage on lake Lac La Nonne, Alberta, with my parents and two older sisters. I then went to college in Calgary and worked in the dental field for ten years. It was then that I was introduced to Marty, through a work acquaintance."

Q: Briefly describe your family farm business and its key players. If you have a business or career "off the farm," tell me about that, too.

A: "My husband is a fourth-generation dryland farmer. My in-laws retired in 2014, so it's solely my husband who oversees all operations. We are so fortunate that his parents still remain an integral part at seeding and harvest times. Working with Marty are two full-time farm employees, as well as additional seasonal workers. In 2002, my husband's parents established a tree farm. Just last year I was able to take the tree farm in a different direction and partner with a Lethbridge restaurant, Mocha Cabana, supplying them with our apples and berries."

Q: What do you consider your primary role?

A: "While Marty is looking after the farm operations I dedicate my time to raising the kids, keeping the business books, managing the tree farm, house, yard, and all that comes with it. "

Q: What is your husband's role in your family and on the farm?

A: "Marty's role encompasses so much. Everything from sales and marketing to agronomy, field planning (seed rotation, fertilizer and chemical application), and money management to coaching our son's hockey team."

Q: What is the best part of life on a farm for you?

A: "Making an income with the people I love most: my husband and children."

Q: Have you started any new traditions in your family that are important to you?

A: "Our infant son passed away in 2013. We have a wildlife reserve that we named in honour of him. Our tradition is to go there to remember him. We visit during different seasons to see the wildlife, whether to find eggs in bird nests, or to track different animal prints in the dirt. It is a special place that we enjoy as a family."

Q: What do you think is a key lesson we can learn from the older generation of farmwives, and what is a great piece of advice you've been given from the older generation that you've valued?

A: "Now that I am in the role of a farmwife, I have a deeper respect for how hard my mother-in-law worked. Additionally, I feel that my husband and I carry on a lot of values from generations past: family is number one; live simply; spend quality time together; work hard; and make sure to pass these values that we are so passionate about on to our kids."

Q: What is a hilarious story you can share about life on your farm?

A: "Date nights. Date nights have changed dramatically ... from being the two of us to the four of us. From fine dining to going for groceries at Costco and farm supplies at Peavey Mart. And we all are excited about it!"

Q: What do you consider the biggest challenge for women entering into / living life on the farm?

A: "In our household, it tends to be a more traditional way of life. There are many times that weather changes, equipment fails, or hours of work change, which means you have to drop or change your plans. Your needs may have to be pushed aside momentarily. Focus on what you have and what you *can* do, not what you can't do."

Q: What is the most important thing you hope your children learn from farm life?

A: "There are so many things to learn on a farm. It's so hard to narrow it down to one thing. I want my children to learn the meaning of roots and the importance of family. I want them to know what it's like to be bored and how to use their imaginations. I want them to know where food comes from, the hard work it takes to grow it, that what we do feeds many people. Also, I want them to respect the land that provides that food."

Q: What are you the most proud of in life?

A: "My most important accomplishment: my family. I hope that our kids will grow up to appreciate what they have been given, being raised on a farm, and to be independent and successful in their endeavours."

Q: For grain farmers, harvest is undoubtedly the busiest time of the year. How are harvest meals managed on your farm? (If you're not a grain farmer, pick an equally busy time of year on your farm and describe how meal times are managed.)

A: "We found that the traditional way of taking meals to the field when everyone ate together was nice, however it created a lot of downtime, especially when there was a time crunch with weather. So I make my warm meal and take it out in disposable to-go containers. Everyone gets a good meal, keeps working, and we estimate that we are done seeding or harvest a few days earlier."

Q: As you know, the demands of farming on your spouse's time is often such that they cannot contribute as much to home or childcare needs as spouses who work forty hours per week can. Describe how the never-ending task of housework is managed in your home.

A: "Maybe because of my dental background I find I get most accomplished when I arrange my time with a work schedule. Certain jobs and tasks are done on certain days or hours of the day. I can keep up with my workload and if all goes as planned, some days I'm ahead. During seeding and harvest, I plan out my meals on a three-week rotation. That way I'm not wasting time deciding what I'm going to be making for meals and I can be organized the evening before."

Q: Having our families eat nutritious meals is becoming more and more a priority for families. Spending less time in the kitchen to achieve that, however, is also a necessity. What is a GREAT recipe your family can share that achieves both of these goals?

A: "My family loves fish, especially trout and salmon. This recipe is great on either."

TROUT OR SALMON MARINADE

1/2 cup light soya sauce
2 tbsp. granulated sugar
2 tbsp. grated ginger root
1 tbsp. olive oil
2 tbsp. lemon juice
2 large garlic cloves, minced (or garlic powder—optional)

Marinate 1–4 hours. Bake at 375 degrees for 20–25 minutes.

INTERVIEW #7: Amy VanderHeide

(*Photo: supplied*)

Age at this writing: 30

Amy is another connection that I have made over social media. She lives and farms in Nova Scotia along with her husband of eleven years, James, and her three sons, aged 8, 4, and 2.

Q: What does the term 'farmwife' mean to you, and do you consider yourself to be one?

A: "To me the term farmwife means the same as "farmer." Yes, you may be providing meals and looking after kids more often than your husband, but you are also a set of hands when needed and often spend days on end out there with your husband getting done what needs doing, plus picking up the slack on other farm jobs that have taken a backseat to harvest yet still need to be done. I think whether you use "farmwife" or "farmer," you are still committed to working on the farm in one way or another. The terminology isn't overly important to me."

Q: Where do you live and how long have you lived there?

A: "I live in the beautiful Annapolis Valley in Nova Scotia. I have lived in Coldbrook for the past eleven years, but I grew up about three minutes away in the small community of Prospect."

Q: What was your background prior to marrying your husband?

A: "I got married at the ripe old age of nineteen, so fairly fresh out of high school, but my background was primarily in agriculture. I spent most of my childhood and teenage years helping my aunts on my grandmother's beef farm. I worked in agriculture-related jobs in high school, at the local zoo (Oaklawn Farm Zoo in Aylesford, NS) and at a farm market. I spent as much time on or around the farm or doing something that involved animals as I possibly could."

Q: Briefly describe your family farm business and its key players. If you have a business or career "off the farm," tell me about that, too.

A: "I live and work with my husband and his parents on a poultry farm, Coldbrook Farms, which is owned by his parents. We farm full time alongside them. We also do crops such as winter wheat, soybeans, and smaller amounts of oats and Triticale. We make a lot of hay to sell to local feed stores as well as selling directly off farm. My husband and I also own a small beef herd that is separate from the poultry farm. The beef farm is called Mountain Base Farm."

Q: How do you think this may differ from the generations before you?

A: "This differs from the generations before me, in my experience anyway, because during the busy season I work the fields, drive tractors, haul hay bales and grain wagons, where the generations before me had the more traditional role of staying home with the children and preparing meals and supporting their husbands that way. Not to say they didn't pitch in when needed, as I know they did their fair share of that as well. For me, I am happiest when I am working alongside my husband in the fields, often with a kid or two in tow as well."

Q: How do you ensure you are not sacrificing your "self" when farm life and work is so time-consuming?

A: "I keep a journal and write in it almost every day, whether it be my thoughts and feelings or things that happened. When I feel like I am losing myself in the chaos I often go back and read through them and it reassures me that yes, this is me, and reminds me of why I made the choice to do this. It kind of keeps me in check. If I notice that things are going off the rails and I am entering a pattern that isn't like me, then I can deal with whatever the situation is a lot easier."

Q: What do you think is a key lesson we can learn from the older generation of farmwives, and what is a great piece of advice you've been given from the older generation that you've valued?

A: "I think a key lesson we can learn from the older generation of farmwives is perseverance. My Grammie is of them, and her mother before her—both super-strong women, though they probably wouldn't acknowledge that of themselves. I take a lot of pride when someone says I remind them of either one of those women. They both lost husbands while they were quite young, yet still pushed on. My aunts helped my grandmother run their beef farm for years after my grandfather passed away; she just persevered. She didn't sell out or stop farming, likely because he wouldn't have wanted her to and because my aunts wanted to keep farming. Still to this day she lives by herself in the farmhouse my mother and her four siblings grew up in. Up until a few years ago she kept watch on the cows at all times. She bakes something every day, does preserves in the summer, and has multiple flower gardens that are, quite simply, masterpieces. And she still keeps everyone in line! She isn't one to give out advice, but she has taught me more than she will ever know just by example."

Q: What is a hilarious story you can share about life on your farm?

A: "I think the funniest thing is when I first started spending more time here I convinced my husband, who at the time was my boyfriend, to let me keep some goats here. Not even useful goats, they were two neutered males. We built them a goat house and a little pen. They'd jump the gate or get their horns stuck in the rails all the time. Now looking back, I have no clue why he ever agreed to having them! He was happy to see them go and much happier when we started to keep cattle, and so was I!"

Q: When it all just seems too much (life, responsibilities, the juggling act) what is something you do for self-care?

A: "Self-care is difficult most of the time ... between the farm and the kids there isn't a lot of "me time." I do like to take bubble baths a lot; they're a great stress reducer and time to enjoy the quiet for me. A good girls' night with friends helps too, even just a quick dinner out or a movie. It gives the brain a break and refreshes me for the next day. Also I always have a good book on the go. It's a great way to escape reality for a while."

Q: For grain farmers, harvest is undoubtedly the busiest time of the year. How are harvest meals managed on your farm? (If you're not a grain farmer, pick an equally busy time of year on your farm and describe how meal times are managed.)

A: "I cook and bake a lot. I love it! Even when it's super busy. My Crockpot is definitely the star of harvest season. Even if it's just to throw a roast or chicken in to go with a quick simple salad, nothing fancy but it's there when we need it. I have also started making big batches of things that can be kept in the freezer and quickly reheated, like single-size burritos or chili divided into smaller batches that can be easily thawed.

Sometimes a quick sandwich in the tractor just has to do, but there is usually something ready in the house to fill stomachs before bed."

Q: Having our families eat nutritious meals is becoming more and more a priority for families. Spending less time in the kitchen to achieve that, however, is also a necessity. What is a GREAT recipe your family can share that achieves both of these goals?

A: "A favourite recipe of ours is one that isn't so well known but is so delicious and features something very Nova Scotian ... apple cider! Cider stew is something I grew up eating. My Nana made it for family dinners and I always looked forward to it. Now in the fall, when the air starts to get cooler, it's the first hardy meal I crave! This can be made on the stove or in the slow-cooker but I will share the slow-cooker version, as it's just as delicious and is easy to leave cooking for the day and come home to a complete meal."

CIDER STEW

2 lbs. beef stew meat cut into 1" cubes

Flour mixture:
3 tbsp. flour
2 tsp. salt
1/4 tsp. pepper
1/2 tsp. thyme

Throw in:

2 cups apple cider (if you can get Boates from Woodville, NS, I highly recommend it!)
2 tbsp. cider vinegar
1/2 cup water
3 potatoes, peeled and quartered
4 carrots, roughly chopped
1 stalk celery, roughly chopped
2 onions, sliced
1 cup peas

Brown beef on all sides in a Dutch oven on the stove. In a small bowl combine the ingredients for the flour mixture. Add the flour mixture to the browned beef and place in the slow-cooker. Throw in the final ingredients and cook on low for 8 hours or high for 4–5hrs. Enjoy with some warm homemade rolls or biscuits!

INTERVIEW #8: Eva Rehak

(*Photo: supplied*)

Age at this writing: 34

FARMWIVES 2

Eva Rehak lives in Saint-Maurice, New Brunswick, and she and her family are going into their eighth season of growing veggies.

Q: What does the term 'farmwife' mean to you, and do you consider yourself to be one?

A: "First, I do not consider myself a farmwife at all and never will. I am a farmer, and proud to be one! I find that farmwife is an old term and there may have been more women who used to only fit in that role. Here in Atlantic Canada, women make up 57.6 percent of new farmers, and I don't believe that any of them would identify as a farmwife rather than a farmer. This year our two employees are also women, so we will be the majority on the farm. That being said, there are still some women today that have married into farm life and have an outside job and do not take on many farm duties."

Q: How long have you been married, and if you have children, how many do you have? Is this your first marriage?

A: "I am not married, but in a way I am, since my partner and I own and operate our farm together and have three kids together as well. Rose-Espérance Eva is 7 years old and was born two weeks after we moved in. Claire Évangeline is 5 years old, and our little man Jakob Alyre is 3 years old. I have never been married before."

Q: What was your background prior to meeting your partner?

A: "I come from a Czechoslovakian background, though I was born in France and moved to Mississauga, Ontario, where I grew up, at 6. In Mississauga there isn't much gardening/farming around—I mainly worked in the restaurant industry—and neither of my parents come from a farming background. To say the least, it is not something I saw myself doing when I got older. I studied Animal Behaviour before attending Collège d'Alfred (better known as Alfred College), which is near Ottawa, and that's where I met Alain. In my first year there I was taking a one-year course to become a vet receptionist. After I finished my year, I stayed and took the Agriculture Technician program. We started going out in my second year at the college."

Q: Briefly describe your family farm business and its key players. If you have a business or career "off the farm," tell me about that, too.

A: "Myself and Alain run a Community Supported Agriculture (CSA) farm with a third partner. We also have two employees helping us this summer. On a little over two acres of gardens and three greenhouses, we grow around fifty kinds of vegetables, as well as some fruit and herbs. Our CSA is twenty weeks over the summer and we also go to the Dieppe Farmer's Market and sell through the Coin Bio/ Organic Corner Cooperative that we created six years ago with three other farms."

Q: What do you consider your primary role?

A: "As a mother of three young children, I have always been the main caretaker. But I also manage the crop calendar, mail the newsletter during the CSA season, as well as helping with fieldwork—mainly transplanting, weeding, and harvesting. I would say that I do half of the paperwork and half the fieldwork."

Q: What is your partner's role in your family and on the farm?

A: "My partner takes care of fieldwork as well, but also does the bed prep—tilling (we have a BCS, no big tractor), fertilizing, creating new beds. He does the fertilizer and equipment ordering. He also takes care of the kids (they love playing wrestling with him), does most of the dishes, and helps with the cooking as well."

Q: Have you started any new traditions in your family that are important to you?

A: "No new traditions per se; it's more a combination of traditions from my Czech background and Alain's Acadian background. Our main mash-up is Christmas. We celebrate on the 24th, like in Czech culture, where we have a supper of fish and potato salad and then wait for Santa to ring the bell. That's when we go and open the presents. Then on the 25th we go over to his family's house and have some more Christmas cheer. We let the kids know that Santa left us presents first, since we are Czech, and then also dropped a few at the other house since he knew we would be stopping by there as well."

Q: What do you think is a key lesson we can learn from the older generation of farmwives, and what is a great piece of advice you've been given
from the older generation that you've valued?

A: "Many. They lived through the beginning of owning/living on a farm
and living without the help of our technology. They have stories to tell
and tricks to be shared. There is an older couple we get our milk from,
and every week I go there I simply watch and listen (and ask a few questions along the way). There is always something new to learn: how to
make your own butter, saving seeds, making preserves, and storing for
the winter. They simply amaze me how much they still do."

Q: What is a hilarious story you can share about life on your farm?

A: "This past summer our youngest was potty training and since we
live on a farm in a rural community I figured let him enjoy the summer
being *free* (no diapers or clothes!). So if you came over to our farm,
Jakob was a wild card. You were lucky to come over and find him
wearing a t-shirt; otherwise, if it was sunny, he was naked. One thing is
for sure, he definitely had the best looking tan in Saint-Maurice—no tan
line whatsoever!"

Q: What do you consider the biggest challenge for women entering into /
living life on the farm?

A: "As a woman in farming I find that there is still a gap—that there are
still a lot of people who, when thinking of a farmer, automatically think
of a man. Yet there are more women starting to farm, with their partner
or even on their own.

For me personally, one of the main challenges is that we started
having kids the first year we started our farm. We tried having help with
day care, but we were not eligible for subsidies. This meant we had the
kids with us at home all the time, so I became the main caretaker and
I was not able to be 100 percent on the farm as we had first intended.

Another challenge, although this one is for everyone, is making it
work and making a living off your farm financially."

Q: What are some ways you try to keep your marriage strong?

A: "Spending time together NOT doing farm things, which is quite hard at times when you pretty much live at your work place, and farming is always on our mind. We try and relax at the end of the day once the kids have gone to bed or go on a walk in the forest. Communication, at times it's hard, but it's key—knowing how the other feels and what can be done to help. And I will also add (it may sound odd) spending time apart. In our case, we work together all day, and so sometimes going away for a day—shopping, seeing friends, attending a farm conference—can be good. You need to miss each other at times as well."

Q: For grain farmers, harvest is undoubtedly the busiest time of the year. How are harvest meals managed on your farm? (If you're not a grain farmer, pick an equally busy time of year on your farm and describe how meal times are managed.)

A: "We are at our busiest starting mid June (we start our CSAs; we are going to two markets already; we are still planting new crops; and also harvesting and weeding), and this goes on until roughly mid September, so lunch needs to be quick and hearty. We simply try and make easy-to-eat meals: salads, sandwiches, or leftovers. I also like to have muffins on hand, a kind of grab-and-go snack. We will be trying something new this year: one of us, including our workers, will prepare the lunch for everyone and each day will be someone different. For a few weeks in the summer we get to have my mom and aunt come for a visit and they usually take care of the meals while they're here."

Q: Having our families eat nutritious meals is becoming more and more a priority for families. Spending less time in the kitchen to achieve that, however, is also a necessity. What is a GREAT recipe your family can share that achieves both of these goals?

SLOW-COOKER PORK SHOULDER

Makes 8 servings

2 onions, thinly sliced
2 cloves garlic, minced

1 can (28 oz./ 796 ml.) diced tomatoes

1/3 cup cooking molasses

1/4 cup cider vinegar

3 tbsp. packed brown sugar

2 tsp. chili powder (I substitute it with sweet paprika)

1 tsp. salt

1/2 tsp. pepper

3 lb. (1.35 kg) pork shoulder

3 tbsp. all-purpose flour

In a slow-cooker, first combine all ingredients, except for the pork shoulder and flour. Top with pork. Cover and cook on low heat for 6–8 hours. Take pork out, whisk flour with ¼ cup water and add to sauce. Cook for thirty minutes on high. Serve pork with potatoes or rice, with sauce on top. Or shred the pork and make it into a pulled pork sandwich.

INTERVIEW #9: Mehgin (Megz) Reynolds

(*Photo: supplied*)

Age at this writing: 31

FARMWIVES 2

My next interview is with a woman who hails from Saskatchewan. I started following her on Twitter about a year ago and have watched her represent farming, farm life, and motherhood with a level of spirit, passion, and honesty that is not often matched. I remember seeing the Premier of Saskatchewan talk about how great she was when she posted a photo of herself harvesting with the caption "Why yes my lipstick does match my combine." She farms with her husband and two daughters, Thea and Rhea.

Although I wasn't sure if she'd agree to being a part of a book with "farmwives" in the title, I asked her anyway, and was thrilled that she was honoured to do so!

Q: "What does the term 'farmwife' mean to you, and do you consider yourself to be one?

A: "Honestly I struggle with the term 'farmwife.' But then, in turn, I feel bad for doing so. There are so many women who are so proud to define themselves by that word and they are so amazing in the ways they take care of and provide for their families. I am secretly a little jealous of the moms and wives that they are.

I identify myself as a farmer, a mom, a wife, an adventure seeker, a blogger (dirtsweatntears.com), an 'agvocator' on Twitter (@farmermegzz), and an amateur photographer. It's a very long list of things that make me who I am, but farmwife is not one of them. To me it's a traditional term that speaks to an amazing mother, home keeper, cook, parts runner, etc. and I usually feel like I am failing at least two of those at any given time. I struggle with being a stay-at-home mom; I wasn't cut out for it. I would rather shovel pigpens out than clean my house since having children ... seriously, who cleans house with two toddlers running around? It's complete mayhem! I will always choose to be in the field, even if I am fixing a breakdown, over being in the kitchen cooking for the crew. I am lucky to have found a husband and a family-in-law that supports me in choosing the role that makes me happiest on the farm and not trying to force me into something more traditional."

Q: Where do you live and how long have you lived there?

A: "We live outside of Kyle, Saskatchewan. I have lived here for five years. I was born in Pincher Creek, Alberta, and grew up in Calgary, Alberta. I lived and worked in Calgary and Vancouver, British Columbia, before meeting my farmer and moving out here."

Q: Briefly describe your family farm business and its key players. If you have a business or career "off the farm," tell me about that, too.

A: "Our family farm is just that: a family farm, and the key players include our two little girls who have spent more time in tractors and combines than I can even total! My husband is a fourth-generation farmer but his dad stopped farming while he was in high school to make beautiful solid oak wood furniture, so when my husband wanted to start farming again it was kind of like starting from scratch with needing to get all the equipment and rent the family farmland. The farm is run by my husband and I, but we have so much help from our parents. His dad helps run and fix equipment when we need a hand and his mom (bless her) does most of the cooking and helps with the girls during seeding and harvest. I like to joke that I need a farmwife to help take care of me and my family while I am in the field. My parents come out from BC for a month or so during seeding and harvest. My mom helps with the girls so they don't need to spend all day in a piece of equipment or at day care, and my dad has learned to seed and combine! My husband and I are a team in every sense of the word. He works off-farm to support us with our farming dreams and I run equipment while he is at work, most often with one or both of the girls with me. When he gets home he switches me out so the girls can have a sit-down supper and fairly consistent bedtimes. We work on equipment together, plan crops and in-crop programs together, and he helps with the house jobs like cooking and cleaning."

Q: What do you consider your primary role?

A: "My primary role is the same as my husband's for the most part: a parent and a farmer. I help run everything but the high clearance sprayer, as that's 'his baby,' and help repair the equipment. I check cows, feed animals, help with haying, though not as much since having kids as the tractors we use are super bumpy and have small cabs. I tend a garden, can and process produce for winter use, and deliver eggs for my girls. They have a farm egg business and all the revenue goes into their university fund."

Q: What is your husband's role in your family and on the farm?

A: "My husband works off-farm to provide for our family and he is the main farmer. He puts more hours in on the farm than I do now that we have kids. He works incredibly hard all the time. He is an amazing father as well, and nothing makes the girls happier than helping Daddy do chores or riding along with him in a tractor or combine. He helps with the cooking and the dishes and in between seeding and harvest there is a good chance he is doing more of the house work then I am."

Q: On some Canadian farms where multiple families are involved, there are a variety of land- and home-ownership complexities that still exist today. In terms of the ownership setup of your farm, is there anything that worries you about your own or your children's security?

A: "We take life insurance policies out for both my husband and I every time we buy land. You can't be too careful when it comes to protecting your family's future. A section of our farm is family land that belongs to aunts and my husband's father; if there was a huge falling out and we lost those acres it would hurt the farm for sure but it wouldn't put us under."

Q: What is a hilarious story you can share about life on your farm?

A: "Last year we bought a bunch of baby chicks to be new laying hens for my girls' farm egg business. All morning we were talking about the "baby chicky poos" that were coming in the mail and my oldest was so excited when we went to pick them up. We took the chicks straight to the farm and got them set up in the brooder house. My oldest came in to see the chicks and was carrying a little plastic toy bath monkey with her. She pet one of the chicks I was holding, looked at the plastic monkey, looked up at me and asked "Mommy, do monkeys have baby chicky poos?"

Q: What do you consider the biggest challenge for women entering into / living life on the farm?

A: "For me, coming from the city, it was the isolation I struggled with the most. Not isolation in the location sense but rather the limited human contact. I made friends but everyone is always so busy farming that it can be weeks or months without sitting down to catch up with friends or have a game night. In the city it was always easy to find someone to go on an adventure with or to meet for a drink."

Q: Is there any piece of advice you wish you had received when beginning your life as a farmwife, and what advice would you give to women marrying into farm life today?

A: "I'm kind of a 'blaze my own trail' sort of a gal, so as much as I always enjoy hearing advice, I take it in turn and do my own thing. The piece of advice I like to give when asked is to find the role that makes you happy on the farm. It's okay if that role isn't traditional, or differentiates from your mother-in-law's; you need to "find your happy," because if you're not happy or fulfilled then your family life will suffer."

Q: What are some ways you try to keep your marriage strong?

A: "I like to surprise him. Sometimes I put on a vintage dress and he comes home to a lovely meal and 1950's housewife, or I dress up in something he loves just for him. He is much more affectionate than I am and it really makes his day when I make a point of giving him a hug or a kiss; it can be when we are out filling the drill or passing in the night, each dealing with non-sleeping babies. It doesn't take much from me to give such a simple thing as a quick kiss, but to him it means so much. We are both so busy that we can go days without seeing each other for more than twenty minutes spread out, so we try to always let each other know that we appreciate each other and everything we are both doing for our family. To us, saying "I appreciate you" can hold much more meaning than saying "I love you.""

Q: What are you the most proud of in life?

A: "This question stumped me for a couple days. I have done so many different things and have so many interests and passions that I really wasn't sure how I could put one accomplishment in front of another. After some soul searching and talking to family and friends the thing I am most proud of is my work ethic and my ability to take on and learn new challenges. I am damn proud of the fact I can float between any job that needs to be done on our farm!"

Q: For grain farmers, harvest is undoubtedly the busiest time of the year. How are harvest meals managed on your farm? (If you're not a grain farmer, pick an equally busy time of year on your farm and describe how meal times are managed.)

A: "I am happiest when I am farming, especially during harvest. There is no place I would rather be than in a combine. In order to make this a reality, I do a lot of meal prep and freezer meals leading up to seeding and harvest so that I can contribute to our meals without having to spend time in the kitchen when we need to be in the field. My mother-in-law does most of the cooking during seeding and harvest and my mother helps as well when she comes out for a month each busy season to help with the girls. I try to pack lunches the night before so every-thing is quick and easy the next morning; rushing out of a house with two girls under three is much like pouring molasses, so the more orga-nized I can be the smoother things run."

Q: When it all just seems too much (life, responsibilities, the juggling act) what is something you do for self-care?

A: "For me my most important self-care tool is exercise. Running is my favourite way to clear my head or think on a problem that needs solving. Thanks to auto-steer I have created modified workouts that I can do in the tractor while seeding—mind you that's only if the girls are not with me. Now that I usually have the girls in the tractor or combine with me, it is such a treat when I get to have time alone by myself!"

Q: Having our families eat nutritious meals is becoming more and more a priority for families. Spending less time in the kitchen to achieve that, however, is also a necessity. What is a GREAT recipe your family can share that achieves both of these goals?

A: "We put in a huge garden every year and then in the fall we do a lot of canning and preserving, making pasta sauces, stewed tomatoes, pesto, and all sorts that really help speed up meal prep during the winter. One of my favourite healthy and fast meals is a chicken dinner in a Crock-pot."

CROCK-POT CHICKEN

I put a whole thawed chicken into a Crock-pot on low in the morning with a little butter and Italian herb rubbed on top. An hour before we intend to eat, I add cut up potatoes and carrots around the chicken, and then in fifteen minutes or so, I top with fresh green beans or asparagus. There is lots of juice to make gravy from the chicken as well!

INTERVIEW #10: Laura Waterfield

(*Photo: supplied*)

Age at this writing: 43

Laura Waterfield is a self-proclaimed "farm girl" who farms with her husband on a grain farm near Kitscoty, Alberta, approximately two hours east of Edmonton. It is the farm her husband grew up on. Since 2013, they've diversified by starting F'Laura n' Company Greenhouse. She and her husband Dean have been married twenty years and have three sons.

Q: What does the term 'farmwife' mean to you, and do you consider yourself to be one

A: "I think being a farmwife involves more than simply being married to a farmer. It doesn't necessarily mean that a woman has to be hands-on in every aspect of the operation, but she has to be "committed" to the farm. For me, farming is not just a way to make a living, it is a way of life, and thus in many ways it defines who I am, and how I view the world. Do I consider myself to be a farmwife? The answer is yes."

Q: What was your background prior to marrying your husband?

A: "I am a farm girl. I grew up on a mixed farm near Spiritwood, Saskatchewan. After graduating from high school in 1991, I attended Lakeland College in Vermilion where I received my diplomas in Animal Health Technology, Herd Health Technology, and a Livestock major. After graduating from college, I worked part time as a veterinary assistant at Weir Veterinary Clinic in Lloydminster, Alberta, for several months before taking a full-time position at Nilsson Brothers Livestock Exchange in Vermilion, Alberta."

Q: Briefly describe your family farm business and its key players. If you have a business or career "off the farm," tell me about that, too.

A: "My husband took over the family farm from his father twenty-three years ago. At the time there was a commercial cattle herd as well as a modest grain operation. Dean and I were both involved with the cattle, but the fieldwork fell mostly on Dean, especially when the boys were small. My father-in-law has always helped us during seeding and harvest, and as the boys have gotten older they have begun to help as well. In 2010, we sold the cattle and switched solely to grain farming. Then, in 2013, we diversified by starting F'Laura n' Company Greenhouse. Today we grow 3,000 acres of cereal, legume, and oilseed crops, and operate 4,600 square feet of greenhouse and 1,600 square feet of nursery space."

Q: What do you consider your primary role?

A: "My role on the farm has changed over the years. I used to help feed livestock, calve cows, and run equipment. Now that there aren't any cattle, and the boys are old enough to help their dad, my focus has shifted. Presently I take care of the financials, and I run the greenhouse operation. One thing that hasn't changed is that my husband and I continue to make farming decisions together."

Q: Have you started any new traditions in your family that are important to you?

A: "Growing up it was just my brother and I in terms of kids. Our closest cousins lived hundreds of miles away, so we missed the opportunity to build relationships with them. The majority of my husband's family live within fifteen minutes of us, which has allowed our boys to spend a lot of time with grandparents, aunts, uncles, and cousins. Even though we see each other regularly, it is important to me that we make a point of getting everyone together several times a year."

Q: On some Canadian farms where multiple families are involved, there are a variety of land- and home-ownership complexities that still exist today. In terms of the ownership setup of your farm, is there anything that worries you about your own or your children's security?

A: "If you had asked me that question two years ago my answer would have been different than it is today. My husband and I knew there were some changes that needed to be made to ensure that myself and our boys would have a future on the farm should something happen to him, but we weren't in a panic to get the ball rolling. Then, in June of 2015, a very close friend and fellow farmer was killed in a tragic vehicle accident. Suddenly it became blatantly obvious to both of us that we needed to get loose ends taken care of immediately. Now, I can say that I feel confident my children and I are secure."

Q: What is a hilarious story you can share about life on your farm?

A: "In the early spring of 2002, my husband and I bought fifty bred heifers. In our area, 2002 was a drought year. We fed them hay and grain all summer. The only bits of green grass were in the ditches, and most of the crops didn't even emerge out of the ground. My husband decided to take on a job long-haul trucking to help make ends meet. That meant that I was left behind to care for 200 cow calf pairs, a four-year-old, and a one-year-old. It goes without saying that when one's husband is away, anything that can go wrong will go wrong. To make matters worse, every one of those heifers was a fence jumper! They got so accustomed to me putting them back in that eventually all I had to do was roll down the truck window and yell. Sometimes, they would jump back over the fence when they saw me coming. About mid July the stress caught up to me, and I got really sick. One day when I was at my worst, a neighbour stopped by to let me know we had cows out. Normally I would have invited him in for coffee, but I was running a fever and my head was pounding. When I heard the news I told him "Tell them to get the *$*#! back where they are supposed to be!" and I shut the door. Some time later I found out that he said exactly what I had told him to, and they did!"

Q: Do you have an app or "hack" to keep yourself organized that you cannot live without?

A: "I am bound to what is on my calendar. In fact, I often joke that if it isn't on the calendar it probably won't happen. With that being said, I reserve the right to rearrange what is on the calendar when it suits me. (No joke)."

Q: Is there any piece of advice you wish you had received when beginning your life as a farmwife, and what advice would you give to women marrying into farm life today?

A: "No, but I have thought often of something my grandma told me before I got married. She said, "Never allow yourself to be in a position where you rely solely on your husband. Make sure you can be independent if you need to be." My grandmother had seen women of her generation widowed or deserted with no means to care for themselves and their children, and she was determined to never be one of those women. For her, the solution was stashing coins away in a coffee can, but women didn't have the same opportunities then that they do today. With her words in mind, my advice to young women marrying into farm life today would be make learning the ins and outs of your operation a priority, regardless of if you work on or off the farm, so that you are capable of making educated farming decisions with your spouse, and on your own if need be."

Q: What are some ways you try to keep your marriage strong?

A: "Farming allows us to spend a lot of time together, but we still try to get away from the farm for a few days every year, just the two of us. We both love to travel, and it gives us an opportunity to experience new things together. I also think it helps that we are working towards a common goal."

Q: For grain farmers, harvest is undoubtedly the busiest time of the year. How are harvest meals managed on your farm? (If you're not a grain farmer, pick an equally busy time of year on your farm and describe how meal times are managed.)

A: "Seeding / greenhouse season and harvest are equally busy times on our farm. I always spend a couple days in spring and fall doing mass-baking and meal prep. I often put meals in the slow-cooker, or pull a dish out of the freezer to put in the oven on days I know I will be rushed."

Q: Having our families eat nutritious meals is becoming more and more a priority for families. Spending less time in the kitchen to achieve that, however, is also a necessity. What is a GREAT recipe your family can share that achieves both of these goals?

A: This is a really difficult question for me because I rarely follow a recipe. I'm a bit-of-this-and-a-dash-of-that kind of gal. My family all enjoy my version of meat pie, so I will share how I make it.

MEAT PIE

I make my pastry from scratch, but ready-made crust from the grocery store will work too. My pastry recipe is enough to make three 9-inch double crust pies, so I triple my filling amount so we can eat one for supper and I have two to stick in the freezer for another day.

For the pastry:

Mix 5 ½ cups flour, 1 tsp. salt, 1 tsp. baking powder together in a large bowl. Cut in 1 lb. shortening. In a 1-cup measuring cup gently beat together 1 egg and 1 tbsp. vinegar, then combine with enough cold water to fill to the 1 cup line. With a fork, mix ¾ cup of the liquid into the dry ingredients so that it forms a dough. If it seems a bit dry, add more liquid as needed. Do not over-mix. Preheat oven to 375 degrees.

For the filling;

You can use any type of meat you wish. It works well with leftover chicken or turkey, and also with ground beef. For each pie I use approx. 3 cups of cooked meat, 1 cup of frozen veggies, 1 cup of diced cooked potatoes or hash browns, ½ a large onion, and 1 can mushroom soup, and salt, pepper, and spices to taste (poultry or beef seasoning).

First, sauté the chopped onion in a large frying pan, then add the frozen veggies, cooked potato / frozen hash browns, and meat. Stir occasionally until the veggies have thawed completely. Next add mushroom soup, salt, pepper, and spices and cook until heated through. Pour the mixture into the uncooked pie shell. Brush the edges of pie shell with the left over egg mixture. Place the top shell on and crimp the edges. Cut slits in the top of the crust to allow heat to escape. Bake for 30–40min. Serve with salad.

Note: I never bake the pies I am freezing before I freeze them. It helps prevent a soggy crust.

INTERVIEW #11: Stephanie Miller

(*Photo: supplied*)

Age at this writing: 36

This next interview is from someone I knew would provide a fantastic perspective to my book celebrating the next generation. I'm biased because I'm lucky enough to have her as a sister-in-law. She's married to my husband's brother, Mike, and I chose her not only because she's a wonderful mother and wife and a talented and driven career woman, but also because of her abilities a great listener and communicator. Stephanie, Mike, and their three children Dane, Aiden, and Sophia, live near Kitscoty, Alberta, where they moved in 2013 to be closer to the Miller Family Farm.

Q: What does the term 'farmwife' mean to you, and do you consider yourself to be one?

A: "For me personally the term farmwife is a way to tell others what your spouse does for a living. 'I'm a doctor's wife,' or 'I'm a military wife,' and so on. My commitment to my husband, who was not a farmer when I married him, is no different now that he farms than when we first married. But do I consider myself to be a farmwife? I consider myself the wife of a farmer. I guess you could say I don't like being defined by what my husband does for a living."

Q: What was your background prior to marrying your husband?

A: "I was and still am a nurse."

Q: Briefly describe your family farm business and its key players. If you have a business or career "off the farm," tell me about that, too.

A: "There is my husband, his dad, and one of his brothers who work together on the farm. My husband also does custom spraying. As for myself, having been a nurse for seventeen years, my role has expanded greatly: from full-time shift work, to management, and now the role of Executive Director. I have built my career on passion and dedication and it has resulted in an award and the executive director position I currently hold."

Q: What do you consider your primary role?

A: "Earning supplemental income."

Q: What is your husband's role in your family and on the farm?

A: "In our home he's an amazing "executive director husband," father, hockey coach, inspiration, and cook. On the farm he's a business owner, entrepreneur, business partner, investor, and labourer.""

Q: Do you ever feel that being a farmwife takes away from any other personal goals you may have?

A: "Absolutely not. I don't see it as being any different than any other committed relationship. I support my husband's goals and he supports mine. We make compromises as needed but never take away from each other's goals."

Q: Have you started any new traditions in your family that are important to you?

A: "Christmas is an important one. We try our best to stay home on Christmas day so we can play with the kids and have some quality time on this special day. It won't be long until they won't want to hang out with us anymore. All we have is now. Also, for one week every summer, when we can take a break from the farm, we spend a week at the lake with the children's grandparents. We fish, swim, get ice cream, ride bikes, and cuddle around the fire. This is a time we all look forward to every year."

Q: Has there been anything in your family or farm life that you've wanted to change?

A: "We (the kids and I) would love to have Mike home more during the busy season (spring, summer, and fall). We all miss having him around. He can be gone from 5 am till 1 am for weeks at a time. This is the reality of running a business dependent on season and weather. It's something we are all aware of and we make the best of it. We make an effort to try and see him for short visits in the evening when we're able."

Q: On some Canadian farms where multiple families are involved, there are a variety of land- and home-ownership complexities that still exist today. In terms of the ownership setup of your farm, is there anything that worries you about your own or your children's security?

A: "We are very fortunate to have had the opportunity to build our home on a quarter of land near the family farm; however our house, which we pay the mortgage for, is on a quarter of land that is under the farm company name. Neither Mike nor I have our names on the company. We did not fully understand at the time of construction that the house that we are paying for legally belongs to the company. If we want the house to be under our name, we would need to buy the quarter section and / or subdivide and buy it from the company. If anything were to happen to Mike and I, the house would not be an asset that our children would acquire.

And if anything were to happen to the company and / or its owners, our house would be considered an asset under the company and we could lose our home. This is a concern as we have witnessed first hand what can happen when the family farm is affected by tragedy."

Q: What is a hilarious story you can share about life on your farm?

A: "Charlie's broken tail. We have a wonderful dog named Charlie. She's a very energetic and lovable chocolate lab. She loves exploring the smells of the outdoors. She's no stranger to water or the passing wild-life, such as deer, elk, beavers, porcupines, skunks and muskrats. One day in early spring, when the ice had finally melted off the dugout, we noticed that Charlie was not her usual bouncy self. She didn't run to see us, her tail wasn't wagging, and to our surprise her tail looked broken! Instead of a straight tail that acted like a whip, Charlie's tail was bent downward from the middle and limp as a wet noodle. "What is wrong with her tail? She can't even sit!" I said to Mike.

Mike took a look at Charlie and decided to palpate her tail. Charlie was not having any of that! If Mike was not holding her collar, Charlie would have taken off. Mike declared, "It's swollen and it hurts her. But I bet she pulled a muscle or something. She's always jumping and chasing stuff. I don't think she broke her tail." Well, what do you do when you need to know the answer to a question? You Google it! Labs are known for loving water, but apparently if a lab swims in icy water they can get "limber tail syndrome," which is a strained muscle (dang it ... Mike was right!). It straightens out and the pain dissipates over a period of a week or so. So not only do I now know what was wrong with our dog's tail and how to treat it, but I also now have my husband's ballooned ego to deal with. But rest assured ... Mikes ego was not swollen for long."

Q: Is there any piece of advice you wish you had received when beginning your life as a farmwife, and what advice would you give to women marrying into farm life today?

A: "The advice I would have liked to have would be 'there is always another piece of large and expensive equipment that needs to be bought. Always.' The advice I would give others is: be independent yet make time for you and your children to be with your spouse. Being a farmwife is a state of mind. It means different things to different people. You are the wife of a farmer, but it doesn't define who you are. Go do what you want and share your successes. Define your role how it suits you."

Q: What are some ways you try to keep your marriage strong?

A: "Date night! At least once a month and / or on the next rain day. Talk about goals and how you plan on reaching them together with support."

Q: For grain farmers, harvest is undoubtedly the busiest time of the year. How are harvest meals managed on your farm? (If you're not a grain farmer, pick an equally busy time of year on your farm and describe how meal times are managed.)

A: "I am so lucky, or should I say my husband and the family are so lucky, to have a mother-in-law and sister-in-law who deliver meals to the fields. Because I work full time and have after school activities to bring the kids to, delivering daily meals to the field is not possible. And if you read above about my husband's role in our home, you will know that he is the cook (specifically during winter months). I can bake, but cooking main meals is not my strong suit. To be honest, when the day comes, I don't see myself ever delivering meals to the fields regularly in the future. That will need some discussion and planning."

Q: Having our families eat nutritious meals is becoming more and more a priority for families. Spending less time in the kitchen to achieve that, however, is also a necessity. What is a GREAT recipe your family can share that achieves both of these goals?

CRUNCHY SALMON CASSEROLE

(This can easily be doubled, tripled or even quadrupled.)

1 large can of salmon
1 1/2 cups of fresh or frozen peas
1 can cream of mushroom soup
1/4 cup breadcrumbs
3 tbsp. of butter
1 small bag of regular potato chips, crushed

Drain can then either remove the bones or crush them into the salmon meat (personal preference). Grease a baking dish. Layer the salmon, then peas, then mushroom soup. Melt butter and mix with breadcrumbs. Top crumb mixture over casserole. Top with crushed potato chips. Bake at degrees for 35 minutes, or until bubbly hot.

(*Photo: supplied*)

Age at this writing: 36

The connection with Jennifer Doelman is another that I made thanks to the wonders of social media. She currently resides outside the village of Douglas, Ontario in _ Renfrew County which is a part of the Ottawa Valley. She and her husband farm her family farm in partnership with her parents.

Here were Jennifer's candid thoughts on the question:

Q: What does the term 'farmwife' mean to you, and do you consider yourself to be one?

A: "'Farmwife' has many meanings to me. Now that I am a wife and a mother, I am the 'keeper of the flock' making sure that my family and my staff have their needs met during planting and harvest especially – field suppers, the logistics of seed and fertilizer, even making sure there is toilet paper in the bathroom!

My paternal grandmother was what I considered to be the traditional 'farmwife.' She raised the children, tended to the livestock and garden and made sure everyone was fed and clothed. A lot of women have downplayed their contribution to the farm and their role as 'keeper of the flock' in saying: "Oh, I'm just a farmwife" but they were the ones that did everything they could to keep groceries on the table and the farm running well. My grandmother used to say 'A well fed man is a happy man.' Years after her death, I would still have customers remark how great Grandma Dick's hospitality was anytime they had been in over the years helping load hay or cattle or simply to buy her eggs.

My mother on the other hand was a full time nurse—but she also worked on the farm. She had to try to be a 'keeper of the flock' AND 'the main bread winner' in the lean, high-interest-rate 1980's. She never identified herself as a 'farmwife' but she was (and still is) a key partner in the farm: she still never missed a night of checking the calves to make sure they were all accounted for, she'd be the one up overnight with the vet helping with a C-section and then head in for a shift at the local nursing home as soon as the sun was up. Having a 'farmwife ' like my mother meant us kids had to be a lot more independent but our strong network of family support meant we were never lacking.

When I was going to university, my grandmother asked me: "Jennifer, are you going to marry a farmer some day?" I replied back:

"Grandma, I'm going to BE a farmer!" I always knew growing up that I would be a full time career woman – but 'farmwife' was never on that list as a goal.

In some ways 'farmwife' is a double standard – can a woman only be a 'farmwife' if she is married to a farmer? Is she a 'farmwife' if she is the unmarried sister who still looks after the meals, the books, the livestock? Is my young mother-in-law who was widowed from a farm accident during harvest still a 'farmwife'? – she still farms but is no longer a 'wife.'

As much as I love the romantic notion of the traditional 'farmwife' – the feminist in me wonders why we only earn the name when we become married. Why do we need a man to earn this title?

That being said, I absolutely LOVE being married to my husband, Mike: he's my best friend, the coolest person in the world, my trusted business partner. But in the end, we're still just 'Mike and Jenn' – he does the laundry if I'm running combine. I'm making suppers if he's running the corn planter – and we are both coordinating staff and customers at the same time while doing these jobs!

Mike and I were married for six and a half years before AJ was born. I wouldn't have identified myself as a 'farmwife' in those days – we were just two people running 80 hours a week, every week, trying to keep up with the demands of our growing businesses.

As soon as I became a mother, I had to somehow figure out what I could actually accomplish at our business and still be a loving wife and nurturing mother. My identity initially took a huge hit – who was I if I wasn't the main operator of our business? I had yearned for so long to be a mother, how could I leave my son with a sitter so that I could still try to contribute to my business? Adding Becky into the mix two years later was even more complicated because my sister-in-law and main business partner had her daughter six months later – neither of us had much of a 'maternity leave' we both had to be back running the business WAY too early while still trying to manage in the sleepless void of postpartum healing!

Maybe for me, the more modern 'farmwife' is just 'any woman in charge of the balancing the home while also being somehow involved in farming'.

Now as the kids become toddlers and preschoolers and our business structures become more defined, I am finally embracing the role of 'farmwife': I make time to make sure that everyone's basic needs are met and enjoy seeing our family and our staff thrive even when exhausted at planting and harvest. I still have an important role in the farm supply business—but now I'm the Chief Financial Officer rather than the main go-to person for everything. I did a good job at it but it was wearing and I really don't miss it. There are several people doing the job now are able to focus exclusively on their roles, and do it better than I. We are all better for the progress made... and, now I can actually prioritize making sure our staff have milk for their coffee and toilet paper in the bathroom!"

Q: How long have you been married, and if you have children, how many do you have? Is this your first marriage?

A: "Mike and I have been married for 10.5 wonderful years. We lost our first daughter, Emily, at 20 weeks gestation due to complications from Turner Syndrome. She was born during planting season so I had to go right back to running our farm supply crop inputs business a couple days after giving birth. It was the hardest thing we have ever had to do. Thankfully we have since been blessed with two beautiful, healthy children (born during the winter to avoid the trials from Emily's pregnancy). AJ, our son, just turned four years old and our daughter, Becky, just turned two. This is the first marriage (and hopefully only!) marriage for both Mike and myself.

Q: What was your background prior to marrying your husband?

A: "The farm we operate is the one I grew up on but it has evolved over the years. When I was young, my parents had a cow-calf operation, a beef feedlot, a retail store to market their beef and a wholesale pedigree seed operation. By the time I attended the University of Guelph for a Bachelor of Science (major: agronomy), my parents had dropped the cattle and the butcher store and focused on turning the seed business into a full service retail crop inputs store. I wasn't sure until I graduated if I was returning to the farm or going into the agri-business industry."

Q: Briefly describe your family farm business and it's key players. If you have a business or career "off the farm"? Tell me about that, too.

A: "Mike and I are farming my family farm in partnership with my parents. We also operate a full-service crop inputs business from our farmstead. The business is called Barclay Dick & Son Farm Supply Ltd (named after my grandfather, Barclay and my father, the '& Son'). It has eight shareholders, including my husband, myself and my parents. The other shareholders include one of my brothers and his wife (she is a manager and agronomist at the business) and our main salesman/agronomist and his wife. The business is very busy and thriving with a young management team and employees. Many key players have young children so it has definitely been a struggle to find balance but it has it's rewards, as well. We are one of the few remaining independent crop suppliers and we service a large and diverse geography."

Q: What do you consider your primary role?

A: "My primary role in our farm supply business is Chief Financial Officer. I have that role as well as lead agronomist and marketer in the farm business. I'm aggressive and fairly good with numbers so it gives me a chance to use my talents but it is a role that also lets me plan my working hours around childcare availability and cropping – more so than when I was primarily customer service."

Q: What is the best part of life on a farm for you?

A: "Living on the farm. Being in rhythm with nature – the blessings (a well-timed rain, a fantastic growing season) and the punishments (drought, ice storms). They allow us to have a better perspective on the cyclical nature of life as well as keeping perspective on our own insignificance.
I love having wide open spaces to work in, play in, and raise our children in. The pride of being stewards of the land. Teaching our children the importance of good stewardship – in our environment and our community."

Q: Do you ever feel that being a "farmwife" takes away from any other personal goals you may have?

A: "Farm life is definitely humbling: I have lived so long with never making plans that I don't realize that it is ingrained in me. You wonder why other people can't understand that RSVP's for events should have a *'we'll be there if it rains'* option. Being a 'farmwife' does have an all-encompassing 'give everything and it's still not enough' lifestyle but it does present opportunities: taking the kids to see Santa in the middle of the work day because there was a break between meetings; suppers at sunset on the tailgate just so the kids can see daddy once today. These are blessings that if we didn't farm I would never even think to take advantage of."

Q: Have there been any "new" traditions that you started in your family that were important to you?

A: "As soon as the crop is planted we load the kids up for a seven-hour drive to see Mike's family. Everyone is just so glad to see us that all of his family and childhood friends plan their weekend to get a visit in – often the only notice they get is a Facebook post as we pull out of our driveway!

We do try to eat once a day as a family- it was something both of our farming families did growing up so it isn't a new family tradition – but now that we finally have children, it's new for Mike and I.

We also try to take the kids to at least one farm show a year so that they get exposure to the industry outside of just our farm. They are still young now but it starts a good habit – it also let's Mike and I touch base with contacts in the industry – and show off our cute kids to a bunch of our college friends we only see at these events."

Q: On some Canadian farms where multiple families are involved, there are a variety of land and home-ownership complexities that still exist today. In terms of the ownership setup of your farm – is there anything that worries you about your own or your children's security?

A: "Farming is a highly capitalized, low margin industry. We have been very active in our succession plan – but even with that wills and partnership agreements become out of date, operating agreements never get finished because we are too busy RUNNING the business that we don't run the business.

I am the eldest of four children: one of my siblings is a business partner in the crop input business but I am the one taking over the family farm.

My husband and I haven't really been paid fair wage because we are 'investing in the farm'. We are full partners who bought into the family business- and have the mortgages to prove it. Unfortunately lately my father keeps talking about needing to be 'fair to the other kids now' – which leaves us wondering what that really means?

My siblings and I are thankfully all on good terms but as my father ages, there appears to be a growing split in how he believes the future of the business should be and where Mike and I want to see the farm head. With everything leveraged to the hilt financially it doesn't give much room for new business ventures or sale of some essential assets. Moving ahead, we need to find some financial autonomy between my parents and ourselves to reduce conflict. We also need to somehow get dad committing to what he wants to do in the next 10 years.

I genuinely worry more about losing our home more to a partnership breakup than to weather or market forces. I also worry that my father's legacy will be a conflict between my siblings and I simply because everyone wasn't on the same page."

Q: What is a hilarious story you can share about life on your farm?

A: "The first wheat harvest after Mike and were married, we put in a long day hauling straw off the field ahead of the rain. My mom brought our whole crew KFC (Kentucky Fried Chicken), which was a pretty rare treat. Unfortunately she underestimated the size of the crew so by the time she got to Mike and I there wasn't much food left. We were exhausted and hungry so when we finished our meagre ration, Mike turned to me to see if I would think less of him for licking the plate off (honeymooners worry about the silliest things) – and caught me doing the same myself!

It was a pretty good icebreaker into the reality of married and farming life – and we made sure that mom went back to the usual routine of burgers or sandwiches for field suppers after that!"

Q: Do you have an "app" or "hack" to keep yourself organized that you cannot live without?

A: "Google calendar:" my phone, my desktop are synced to it – I set reminders so that I can stay on top of everyone's appointments: business meetings, family appointments , my **parents'** appointments, even corn loads to Greenfield Ethanol!

My phone IS my workstation—with it, I can run/access just about anything: emails, crop scouting – take a picture of the insect chewing on the soybeans, ordering parts – I have all the serial numbers saved on a spreadsheet that I can access through the Dropbox app so I have literally been able to order parts for the combine while picking up groceries!"

Q: What do you consider the biggest challenge for "women" entering or living life on the farm?

A: "1. Being treated as equals – by our peers as well as setting those standards for ourselves.

My father prides himself on being a progressive man yet my male siblings were always paid better than I was, even with less education and less experience. His logic was always 'the boys needed more help, you have your life together, they don't' – which never made sense to me but he was the one who set the wages then.

As a consequence of this, I do regularly double check that our staff are on parity for wages based on their skillset, education and responsibility no matter their gender.

2. Learning to stand up for ourselves: When the salesman drives in and asks: "Is the boss here?" You say: "Sure! You're looking at her!" and stand there holding your own until he is ready to treat you as an equal rather than: *"just the farmwife"*.

Q: Is there any piece of advice you wish you had received when beginning your life as a farmwife – and, also what advice would you give women marrying into farm life today?

A: "Since I was born and raised on the farm I wasn't naïve to life on the farm but I have a lot of new 'farmwife' friends who have suffered severe culture shock.

My advice for women who aren't used to farm life is:

"Be patient. Mother Nature sets the pace on the farm. Your partner/your staff/your livestock aren't trying to wreck your plans/cash flow on purpose – things happen outside of anyone's control.

Have an open discussion with your partner and be clear about your frustrations but don't just blame him outright – you are both going to have to learn to adapt to this new partnership.

But if you watch for the opportunities: tailgate suppers, finishing harvest moments before the rain starts pouring down, combine rides with daddy, you will be so much richer for being a part of this crazy farm life."

Q: What is the most important thing you hope your children learn from farm life? If you don't have children, what is the most important lesson you have learned?

A: "I want my children to learn that they are important but that the entire world doesn't revolve around them – Christmas presents get opened after chores, a dry summer means a lean winter. For Mike and I, these were the lessons that taught us humility and gratitude growing up on the farm.

Farming life allows you to be aware of the cycles of life: the rebirth of spring, lazy hazy days of summer, the energization of fall harvest and the quiet hibernation and rest period of winter. We put in long days but we have the privilege of being in tune with nature. I am starting to realize that maybe more humans could be happier if they paid more attention to the world around them instead of getting caught up in the artificial lifestyles we have created for ourselves."

Q: What are ways you try to keep your marriage strong?

A: "1. We try to kiss each other good morning and good night every day. A pat on the bum when trading off as combine operators or a quick "I love you" as we are heading out to different jobs for the day – just a whole lot of little things to make sure they become a big thing.

2. Genuinely taking time to appreciate the your spouse's contribution to the farm and doing what we can to help make each other's day a little easier.

3. Making sure we pay for a babysitter once in a while so that we have an evening with a little less "kids and work talk" and more just "Mike and Jenn" talk: music, movies, planning future holidays together. Just making sure that we still actually like each other and aren't just convenient roommates.

Q: For grain farmers – "harvest" is undoubtedly the busiest time of the year. How are harvest meals are managed on your farm? (If you're not a grain farmer – pick an equally busy time of year on your farm and describe how meal-times are managed)

A: "'Spring rush' is an intense period of time from mid-April to mid-June where we and our staff regularly put in superhuman hours, 6 days a week: I try to have sandwich foods, fruits, veggies & granola bars for the staff to grab as they go through the break-room.

If an employee is working past supper time, we feed them: often sandwiches or burgers – food you can eat in the tractor seat. I try to take a half an hour late in the afternoon to put together meals for everyone who is likely staying late, pick the kids up at daycare and then do a 'milk run' to everyone in the field. Cell phones are great because the guys can text if they need more seed or fertilizer or a tool for a quick repair while I'm going out to them. The kids like helping (usually) and that's why I joke we can't have any more kids—you can't pull a gravity wagon with a minivan!

I stock back up on the foods after I drop the kids off at daycare in the morning – often a parts run at the same time because you can't waste a good trip into town!"

Q: Having our families eat nutritious meals is becoming more and more a priority to families. Spending less "time" in the kitchen to achieve that, however, is also a necessity. What is a GREAT recipe your family can share that achieves both of these goals?

A: Tacos! I use lean ground beef or ground chicken plus a can of black beans to increase the fibre. Brown the meat, mix in the beans, a large onion & a low sodium taco mix. It's very filling and satisfying. I make a few pounds at once so it's good for a few days.

The first night we make soft shelled tacos (I buy the whole grain pre-packaged ones) loaded with green peppers, tomatoes, lettuce, cheese, salsa and low fat sour cream.

The second day we can make nachos or taco salad (also loaded with veggies). Everyone finds something in it they like.

If there is still more meat mix left another meal it can make is Mexican Sloppy Joes mixed with salsa and put on a hamburger bun.

They aren't leftovers if you plan for them! They are 'planned overs'

Most Sundays I make a big dish of something that lasts until mid-week as lunch or supper options.

This Christmas my parents got us a panini maker so I'm thinking there will be a lot more interesting sandwiches this planting season!

INTERVIEW #13: Lynn Prevost

(*Photo: supplied*)

Age at this writing: 53

FARMWIVES 2

Lynn Prevost is someone I came across via social media. She is an active 'ag-vocate' of the farming life, and of the people who do it! I was finally able to meet her in person in November 2016, and I'm thrilled she agreed to take part in this book. She lives near Rose Valley, Saskatchewan, where she's lived for the last twenty years.

Q: What does the term 'farmwife' mean to you, and do you consider your-self to be one?"

A: "The term farmwife is taken too lightly, I find. I really do prefer the "Farmher" title, taken from a business woman in the United States. I also like to be referred to as a "Harvesther," I feel that farmwife really does not hold the title it should. Farmwives do far beyond what they are given credit for."

Q: How long have you been married, and if you have children, how many do you have? Is this your first marriage?

A: "This is not my first marriage. We have been married for thirteen years. We are a blended family of five children. Two are mine, and three my husband's."

Q: Briefly describe your family farm business and its key players. If you have a business or career "off the farm," tell me about that, too.

A: "Our farm business just recently formed a partnership with my step-son to incorporate him into farming. We are a grain farm with no animals other than a dog and cats. My husband and I also have a custom harvesting business known as "Prevost Harvesting." We travel into the United States and harvest wheat and other crops and work our way back into Canada."

Q: What do you think the primary difference is between the younger gen-erations of farmwives and the women that came before them?

A: "Farmwives from generations prior had to do more physical labour than we do know. The machines on the farm have advanced so much. I am not saying that farmwives do not work hard because I know they do. The generation before used to farm smaller farms; this generation has larger farms with less help. We still work hard trying to get everything done, we are just fortunate to have machines to help get those jobs done faster and easier."

Q: What do you consider your primary role?

A: "My role on the farm is Bookkeeper, Gardenher, Housekeeper, Cook, Gopher (go for this and for that). I also run the tractor/grain cart for harvest and our harvest business and work for the Association of Canadian Custom Harvesters Inc. as the Executive Secretary."

Q: Has there been anything in your family or farm life that you've wanted to change?

A: "I wish there was more family get-togethers. I do realize though that with a blended family and all five children with partners, time needs to be shared."

Q: What is a hilarious story you can share about life on your farm?

A: "A funny story of me learning to operate the tractor/grain cart was my first time unloading into the truck. The hired man (who had more patience to teach me than my farmer husband did) went with me for one cartful. He then jumped out of the tractor to guide me in filling the truck. I had the chute of the cart wide open (it had to be because it was coming out full speed). He was signalling to me to back up and fill the front hopper of the semi. I put it in reverse and oh my, did I reverse! I just about knocked him off the truck, and filled the stacks of the truck with grain along with the hood of the truck. My husband came with a full hopper in combine to see what was wrong, took one look at what I had just accomplished and went back towards the field and sat there until I came to him."

Q: On some Canadian farms where multiple families are involved, there are a variety of land- and home-ownership complexities that still exist today. In terms of the ownership setup of your farm, is there anything that worries you about your own or your children's security?

A: "We are a blended family, therefore there is always concern. I want things to be fair to all of them. I can only pray and hope that how we have decided that things should be looked after when we are gone are met. My biggest fear is fighting amongst the children when we are gone. I worked for a lawyer in my days before farm life and have seen too often what can happen over greed. When I left my husband I walked away with nothing. At that time I was looking for my happiness, not money. If more people realized that money does not buy happiness, this world would be a much better place to live.

Q: What are some ways you try to keep your marriage strong?

A: "Keeping a marriage strong is sometimes tough when times are tough. Communication is a key ingredient ... not that I always use that key. Do things together off the farm. Learn to let go of things you have no control over."

Q: When it all just seems too much (life, responsibilities, the juggling act) what is something you do for self-care?

A: "I enjoy many hobbies and some of them I would like to do more often. I enjoy taking photos, spending time with family and friends, crafting. I also enjoy being outdoors (when the weather is nice)."

Q: Having our families eat nutritious meals is becoming more and more a priority for families. Spending less time in the kitchen to achieve that, however, is also a necessity. What is a GREAT recipe your family can share that achieves both of these goals?

A: "I have a few go-to meals when we are on harvest, and I am in the field the same amount of time as the rest, so I LOVE my Crock-pot! When the garden comes off, this is one of my favourites."

ZUCCHINI QUICHE

4–5 cups of grated zucchini
4–5 beaten eggs
1/2 cup canola oil
1 small onion, chopped
1 1/2 cups grated cheese
salt and pepper to taste

For the flour:

1 cup of Bisquick mix (or 1 cup of flour and 1 tsp. baking powder)

Add and stir one ingredient at a time into a large mixing bowl until all ingredients have been mixed together. Pour into the pastry base (in a greased quiche pan or casserole dish) and bake at 350 degrees for 30–40 minutes. I serve with a salsa and a salad.

(*Photo: supplied*)

Age at this writing: 37

Crystal Schnarr and her husband are dairy farmers from just outside of Elnora, Ontario. They have lived on the "home farm" location for nine years. They have five children, aged 14, 13, 9, 5 and 4. They've been married for seventeen years.

Q: What does the term 'farmwife' mean to you, and do you consider yourself to be one?

A: "Farmwife means being there to support my spouse, as well as the business, in any way possible. Now that I've got all of my minions in school, it is a bit more of a reality in the sense that I can physically help with chores, tractor work, or parts and lunch running. I am definitely a farmwife. I have adapted myself to the position and am so happy."

Q: Briefly describe your family farm business and its key players. If you have a business or career "off the farm," tell me about that, too.

A: "We own and operate a dairy farm. In 2014 we built a brand new barn and installed two robotic milkers. We went from tie stall, twice-a-day milking to this new, more efficient, easier-on-the-knee system and are happy we did so. The key players in the farm are my husband and father-in-law. The farm was originally my father-in-law's parents' farm, but at a different location. He moved the farm here from the Waterloo region in 1976 along with my mother-in-law. In my spare time I sell an all-natural line of health and beauty products called Heaven Scent Natural Products."

Q: What do you consider your primary role?

A: "For sure stay-at-home mom / homemaker. Hubby makes sure the barn is in order; I make sure the household stays in order. And we help each other in both of those departments as well. You've got to work together and give and take a little."

Q: What is your husband's role in your family and on the farm?

A: "In our family, my husband is the sole 'money maker' (if there is such a thing on the farm), and that father figure for the children. On the farm, he is one of the key decision makers and doers. He takes a bigger role in the field planning / work, but is still very involved with the herd."

Q: Do you ever feel that being a farmwife takes away from any other personal goals you may have?

A: "For sure it does. I think having a family does too. We all have that 'dream job' or something we would want to do if there were no obstacles. Since my youngest has started school, I've been considering what to do, and if off-farm work is something that is doable, and if so, what it might be. There are certain jobs I'd love to do, but they would pull me away from my family at the wrong times. I always think: Maybe some day, but maybe not. God has put me right here, right now, for this purpose, and I'm happy with that."

Q: What is a hilarious story you can share about life on your farm?

A: "Perhaps not hilarious, but I remember one New Year's Eve, my husband went up to the barn to do the final barn check before we rang in the new year. Well, it turned out that a pipe had burst in the dairy and there was water everywhere. Needless to say it was something that required immediate attention and repair. I remember him running (literally) down to the house with seconds to spare before the new year was officially here. We 'Happy New Year'd,' kissed, hugged, and he ran (literally) back up to the barn to finish his work. There are of course many other little things like this that happen on a regular basis, and I think that we need to laugh at and enjoy every moment we have."

Q: What are some ways you try to keep your marriage strong?

A: "We talk, a lot, all the time. We check in daily with each other, even if it's in the tractor or barn. We try to make it a point to get out for a date night at least once a month to catch up and focus on us."

Q: What are you the most proud of in life?

A: "As a stay-at-home mom, it often feels like nothing has been accomplished and there isn't a big thing in life to be proud of. Reflecting on it, though, I've got five children who are decent human beings with our faith system ingrained in their hearts, a household that runs relatively smoothly, and a relationship with a man who loves me with all my faults and failures. All this without a manual, or instructions."

Q: For grain farmers, harvest is undoubtedly the busiest time of the year. How are harvest meals managed on your farm? (If you're not a grain farmer, pick an equally busy time of year on your farm and describe how meal times are managed.)

A: "I typically make and send them out. I've got some awesome children who love to help, and it's usually an all-hands-on-deck activity. I make the main part of the meal and the kids get the drinks and snacks, and help with the packing."

Q: When it all just seems too much (life, responsibilities, the juggling act) what is something you do for self-care?

A: "I like to crochet. It brings calm and time to sit down. I also really really love to bake, especially with my children. Some people see it as a chore, but I really do think it's therapeutic."

Q: Having our families eat nutritious meals is becoming more and more a priority for families. Spending less time in the kitchen to achieve that, however, is also a necessity. What is a GREAT recipe your family can share that achieves both of these goals?

LASAGNE & CAESAR SALAD

I make a simple lasagne. I use oven-ready noodles. Cook a pound of beef (I cook mine in a Tupperware Stack Cooker container in the microwave). Add a jar or two of pasta sauce and cottage cheese into the beef. Put a bit of sauce saved from the jar into the bottom of the pan, then layer the noodles, sauce mixture, and mozzarella cheese until you get to the top of the pan, ending with cheese. Cover and cook at 400 degrees for 45 minutes. Remove foil and cook for 15 minutes.

I like to make mine ahead of time, so the noodles then have time to get soft. The key to busy households is to plan ahead and make sure you've got something easy or made ahead for those busier days. Casseroles and Crock-pots are my friend!

INTERVIEW #15: Kimberly Ducherer

(Photo credit: Blake Loates Photography)

Age at this writing: 32

Kim Ducherer is another one of those "rock star" women defining their own roles on their farms and creating the lives that make them happy. She was referred to me from an old colleague of mine, and since I've gotten to know more about her I'm convinced she is the perfect example to raise two future young women. Kim and her husband of ten years farm in Leduc County, Alberta, with their seven- and five-year-old daughters. They've lived in their current home since October 24, 2007, when, in her words: "We moved in after building it ourselves. It was 147 LONG DAYS in our fifth wheel together before we moved in. Thankfully we didn't have kids yet!"

Q: What does the term 'farmwife' mean to you, and do you consider your-self to be one?

A: "A farmwife is someone who is the wife of a farmer. It means you're on call 24/7, have an open mind, and are always willing to learn and do new things. To me, the closest profession to a farmwife is a mother: it's a never-ending job with low pay and long hours, but the lifestyle is intangible and the rewards last forever."

Q: What was your background prior to marrying your husband?

A: "I met my husband when I was seventeen in my last year of high school in New Sarepta, Alberta. I went to college for small business and entrepreneurship when we'd been together two years. I graduated with honours in June 2005 and we were married on August 5, 2006."

Q: Briefly describe your family farm business and its key players. If you have a business or career "off the farm," tell me about that, too.

A: "Our farm includes 150 head of cattle and about 900 acres of grain land (rented) and another 600 acres of hay land we put up, plus pasture land. Calving starts in February and overlaps into seeding, then we start with the first cut of hay, hauling pairs to pasture, second cut of hay, harvest, hauling bales home and bringing the cattle back to the home quarter. That takes us to around November, and we start again in the new year. When I'm not farming, I'm running my business Farm Wife Style. I'm a jewellery designer and my pieces were selected to be in the Grammy and Oscar gift bags in February 2016, which gave my business a lot of notoriety. I have since designed another collection and successfully launched it in Canada to my twenty plus retailers. I'm working on my second collection and getting into the US market."

Q: What do you consider your primary role?

A: "My primary role is making sure my family is taken care of. I wear so many hats all with that same goal. Regardless of whether I have to be awake early to cut hay or help with a calf, get our daughters to school, pack orders, or meet with a new retailer, my end game is still the same. I need and want to provide for my family to help us live the best life possible."

Q: How do you think this may differ from the generations before you?

A: "I think one of the only differences between a farmwife in 2016 and a farmwife in years past is technology. A lot of what we do now is with larger, more intricate machinery and the learning curve is a bit steeper than it would have been before, but the time and manual labour saved is well worth it. I can't help but say a prayer of thanks every time I load my dishwasher or washing machine as well. Without those kinds of advancements, I wouldn't be able to help out as much outside with the actual farmwork because I would be inside washing by hand. The days would be a lot longer than they are and I wouldn't have had the opportunity to start Farm Wife Style."

Q: What is your husband's role in your family, and on the farm?

A: "My husband and I are even when it comes to parenting. We're both able to be home for our girls but I do participate in a bit more of their activities and school responsibilities than he does, simply because he's more efficient than I am with the equipment and chores. He takes the lead on the farm and I follow his direction. He's also a meat cutter and has a shop on our property for his hunting clients every year. It's not inspected so we don't sell our own meat, but it's definitely handy to have a husband who knows how to butcher our own animals as well."

Q: How do you ensure you are not sacrificing your "self" when farm life and work is so time-consuming?

A: "This is definitely more difficult during the summer and fall months when haying and harvest are going on, because we are at the mercy of the weather and when you need to go, you need to go and the days are long. Since my farm life and my work life overlap and intertwine, I'm lucky to have my business as a representation of my whole self. There's not a day that goes by where I'm not thinking of the next design, piece, or collection I want to create, regardless of whether I'm in my office or in a tractor."

Q: Do ever feel that being a farmwife takes away from any other goals you may have?

A: "There are times when I feel like it detracts from my personal goals because it's so time-consuming, but for the most part, my business has grown with me as a farmwife; I've worked it into my life and am fortunate enough to share it with the rest of the world without the commitment of the farm taking away from it."

Q: Have you started any new traditions in your family that are important to you?

A: "What I would love to start with my family are sleigh rides. I grew up around horses and have always loved them. I would love to get a draft team and wagon and take my family for sleigh rides all year round; it's a dream I'm getting closer and closer to every year. As for currently, our family carries on the traditions we were raised with: watching *Christmas Vacation* and *Home Alone* on snowy December Saturdays, decorating our house for Christmas while watching the Grey Cup, reading *The Polar Express*, having family dinners at Easter, Thanksgiving, and Christmas, and we always go camping for the July long weekend, since it's my birthday, as well as the May, August, and September long weekends."

Q: What is a hilarious story you can share about life on your farm?

A: "My husband rarely ever puts anything back where it came from. He takes it out, uses it, and drops it where he's done with it. When the snow melts, we find tools all over our yard, and one year I even tripped on a ladder that was lying in the middle of the yard under two feet of snow. I was yelling and swearing when it happened, but I think about it now and how funny it must have looked and I laugh."

Q: What do you consider the biggest challenge for women entering into / living life on the farm?

A: "Not losing yourself in the chaos of farm life. There's so much going on at any time that it can be easy to just keep going, task after task, but at the end of the day when all the chores are done, the kids are fed, the homework and laundry are done, did you take time for yourself? The only way you can take care of your family and farm is if you take care of yourself first and make sure your cup is full."

Q: What are some ways you try to keep your marriage strong?

A: "Working with your spouse is NOT easy. When it's busy, we get angry and / or frustrated with each other seventeen times an hour. It's so difficult to remember that during the day we're colleagues and when we get home we're spouses. A good night's rest is crucial; without sleep we're both grumpy jerks. Next is food. I get HANGRY so easily, so I know if I haven't eaten my temper is short. Once we do both of those things, we try really hard to laugh with each other and spend time together, even if it's just watching half a movie when the kids have gone to bed. Most weekends we go out for family supper, but we also leave our kids with their grandparents often to enjoy each other's company."

Q: What are you the most proud of in life?

A: "This is a hard one! I am so proud of so many things I have accomplished in this life—a successful ten-year (and counting) marriage, two beautiful, healthy, happy, intelligent children, a home that we built with our own two hands, a strong and healthy relationship with my parents and sister, still driving the hot rod my dad and I built together, and definitely Farm Wife Style. Using all the skills I have acquired in life to dream big and successfully launch and grow my business are second to not a lot in my life."

Q: When it all just seems too much (life, responsibilities, the juggling act) what is something you do for self-care?

A: "Take a break. There's always got to be something to look forward to, especially when you're a farmer, because life gets hectic and crazy. Every year my parents, friends, and I drive our hot rods to Radium for a car show; it's the highlight of my year. My husband goes away hunting with his friends in November and he loves that break. We try to take a family vacation every year in the winter to somewhere warm and spend time together before coming back to start up calving season. Life is all about having fun! Make sure you take the time for yourself to regroup and recharge."

Q: Having our families eat nutritious meals is becoming more and more a priority for families. Spending less time in the kitchen to achieve that, however, is also a necessity. What is a GREAT recipe your family can share that achieves both of these goals?

A: "One of my favourite meals (and a tradition in my family for Christmas Eve) is clam chowder and homemade buns. My mom makes the best, and now I do too!"

CLAM CHOWDER

Serves 6-8 adults

1 cup ham or bacon, chopped
1 cup onion, chopped
1 cup celery, chopped
2 cans (10 oz each) baby clams, not drained
6 cups milk
1/2 cup flour
1/2 cup cold water
2 large potatoes, chopped or shredded
2 large carrots, chopped or shredded

Fry bacon/ham in a large pot, add celery and onion and cook until onions are clear. Add cans of clams, and liquid and let some of the liquid cook off. Stir constantly. Add flour and water to a shaker cup or jar and shake together. Add milk and bring to boil.

Once boiling, add flour mixture to pot and stir constantly until it thickens. Add potatoes and carrots and reduce heat to low. Simmer on stove until ready to eat.

(*Photo: supplied*)

Age at this writing: 39

Katie MacLennan lives with her husband and twelve-year-old son near West Cape, Prince Edward Island in eastern Canada. She and Jonathan have been married for eighteen years. Farming has been in both her and her husband's families for generations but when I asked her **"What does the term 'farmwife' mean to you, and do you consider yourself to be one?"** her answer was not traditional.

Q: What does the term 'farmwife' mean to you, and do you consider yourself to be one?

A: "It feels old fashioned. I think of my grandmother. The years of love and commitment that she put into my grandfather's family farm. They were partners in everything, but back then the farms were considered to be run by the men and the women played the supporting role. When I was first married I went to a meeting with my mother-in-law. The group was called, "Women in support of Agriculture." That name bothered me, and it still does now. It should have been called "Women in Agriculture." I want to see women celebrated for being a part of agriculture. I never refer to myself as a farmwife just as I don't refer to Jonathan as a farm husband. We are a team, and our farm wouldn't work any other way."

Q: What was your background prior to marrying your husband?

A: "I grew up with two older brothers. Our mom was a full-time Registered Nurse, and our father also worked in the health care system here on PEI. When they both retired they bought the local country store."

Q: Briefly describe your family farm business and its key players. If you have a business or career "off the farm," tell me about that, too.

A: "Jonathan and I own MacLennan Properties Ltd. We grow 700 plus acres of processing and seed potatoes, as well as 550 plus acres of grain and oil seeds, and 600 plus acres of hay. I am the last of my family to be farming and I take a lot of pride in that. It is our hope that our son Gabriel will want to continue on."

Q: What do you consider your primary role?

A: "I work full time on the farm alongside Jonathan and our crew. I am everything, from running the whole operation when Jonathan is away on business, to chief cheque writer, but my primary roles are Bookkeeper and co-Operations Manager. Since coming onto the farm nineteen years ago I have grown to absolutely love my job and look forward to it every day. There are pros and cons to every job, but the major pro I has been the ability to be a stay-at-home mom for our son and pick and choose, most of the time, when I work. I don't have an off-the-farm job, but it has given me the chance to be involved in many volunteer positions in our community, the main one being the Home & School Association at my son's school."

Q: What is the best part of life on a farm for you?

A: "I don't think I can pick just one. The pride I feel knowing that we are helping to feed the world. The pride I feel every year when the seed goes in the ground, and watching it grow. Then in the autumn, watching what our months of toil, labour, and love have produced. That happy heart feeling I get when I hear Gabriel telling people that he's going to farm when he grows up. The feel of fresh soil that has been worked in spring between my bare toes. The pride I feel when I think of not only Jonathan's family history on this farm, but my own family farm history, and knowing how proud my grandparents would be. Most of all, getting to work beside my best friend every day, and loving the life I chose."

Q: On some Canadian farms where multiple families are involved, there are a variety of land- and home-ownership complexities that still exist today. In terms of the ownership setup of your farm, is there anything that worries you about your own or your children's security?

A: "Having to worry about multiple children receiving what is rightfully theirs is not something we have to worry about as we have one child. I think what worries me is our son continuing to farm in the state of the industry as it sits right now. Every year it gets harder and harder to justify to the public why farming is so important. There is so much backlash for all farmers, and we seem to spend an incredible amount of time defending our industry and farming practices. The misconception from much of the public is enough to encourage your children not to farm. That is what worries me."

Q: Has there been anything you were not prepared for since becoming a farmwife?

A: "Hahaha, I think back to our first crop of potatoes as a married couple. That first fertilizer bill I opened up—well, a little voice in my head wanted to scream, "WHAT THE HELL HAVE I GOTTEN MYSELF INTO?!" Of course Jonathan laughed and said, "Dear, get used to it." The cost of farming is something I wasn't prepared for."

Q: What do you think is a key lesson we can learn from the older generation of farmwives, and what is a great piece of advice you've been given from the older generation that you've valued?

A: "My mother-in-law has taught me so much about being a farmwife: patience and flexibility for one; the farm depends so much on Mother Nature. There are times when plans are made, trips are planned, or just a quiet evening at home is needed, but a turn in the weather or a telephone call from your customer can change everything. This is guaranteed to happen, without a doubt.

Do not depend on men to fix anything or build anything in the home or around it. This is not a bad thing at all. In the nineteen years I have been married, I have become one with my toolbox and the Yellow Pages. Time does not get taken away from the farm for that silliness. It pushes you to fix things yourself or find someone to build it, and I love that.

Priority has to be the farm: that is the breadwinner 100 percent of the time—it has to be. I will say this though: Jonathan is one heck of a mouse hunter, just not during digging season. And last but not least, love the way diesel, the grinder, and potatoes smell, because you are going to be smelling them for the rest of your life."

Q: What is a hilarious story you can share about life on your farm?

A: "This happened a few years after Jonathan and I took over the main operations of the farm. I had been working around the farm for quite some time and we were into harvest season. We had lots of machinery out being used and one of them was the skidsteer. We used it around the warehouses to clean up dirt and rocks. Well, I got it into my head that I wanted to learn how to drive it. I had already learned how to drive all the tractors, trucks, and forklift, so I thought I needed to accomplish this. So one of the farmhands who had been around since before Jonathan was born said he would show me. A quick lesson later and I was off. I was a pro—this was easy! What could go wrong? Well, while I was doing sharp left and right turns I failed to remember that I had a large potato bucket attached to the front, and also failed to remember that I was getting close to the side of our shop. One quick turn right and I ripped a big hole in the side of our shop at the exact same time my father-in-law drove into the yard. Panic set in and that same farmhand looked at me laughing. He said, "You keep him distracted and I'll go get a sheet of steel in building." After the hole was patched I was still upset. He then showed me the other fifteen patches on the same wall of the shop that he had repaired over the years, and called each by the name of the person who put it there. To this day I'm still only at one."

Q: What are some ways you try to keep your marriage strong?

A: "Communication. When you work beside someone day in and day out and then go home with that same person you need to communicate about anything and everything. For Jonathan and I, we spent the first eight years of our marriage and farm life without children. We spent 90 percent of our time together and we wanted that. To this day Jonathan is the person I want to spend all of my time with. Our relationship is something we have made number one from the beginning. I remember many late nights being his co-pilot in the tractor because that would be the only way I would see him that day. I'm not saying it was easy, especially in the beginning. I was three months in to being twenty-one when we married, and there was a lot of maturing that still needed to happen, which caused lots of miscommunications, and a few tears. Eventually I stopped saying "I'm fine," when asked how I was feeling and started telling him how I was actually feeling. So COMMUNICATION is everything."

Q: For grain farmers, harvest is undoubtedly the busiest time of the year. How are harvest meals managed on your farm? (If you're not a grain farmer, pick an equally busy time of year on your farm and describe how meal times are managed.)

A: "As potato farmers harvest time would definitely be our busiest time, with planting time a close second. During the weekdays the lunches are packed in the morning during the "go time" hour. That's when everyone is getting up and ready for school and work. For supper I try very, very hard to have a hot meal going to the field for the three of us. I have made it my mission during this time of year, since Gabriel was born, to make sure Jonathan and he get to see each other at least for that time. The older Gabe has gotten the more time he spends in the field, especially in the evening and on weekends. Sometimes it works, sometimes it doesn't. I don't cook for the staff like my grandmother did. It is easier for everyone to bring their own. With allergies and timing it just wouldn't work. I do however usually provide a supper or two during planting and harvest, usually on a Saturday evening, and it's always hot."

Q: Having our families eat nutritious meals is becoming more and more a priority for families. Spending less time in the kitchen to achieve that, however, is also a necessity. What is a GREAT recipe your family can share that achieves both of these goals?

A: "Well I'm all about Prince Edward Island and the amazing food we produce here so ... Sunday Supper! That's PEI baked potato, island-raised beef—either strip loin, or rib eye steak, and (in the spring or fall) fresh-caught PEI Lobster."

PEI SUNDAY SUPPER

PEI Baked Potato:

1 perfectly grown PEI Russet Burbank Potato, topped with a good serving of ADL butter (the real thing, not margarine), a generous dollop of ADL sour cream, a handful of ADL old cheddar cheese, shredded, and freshly-cooked bacon bits. Cook your potatoes in the oven at 400 degrees for 45–50 minutes.

PEI Beef:

Get your favourite cut of PEI steak, add salt and pepper, rub
a garlic clove over both sides, drizzle with olive oil, then
pop it on the barbecue. Remember: LOW and SLOW.

PEI Lobster:

It is so much better to get fresh live lobster and learn to cook it
yourself. So in a big Crock-pot, fill it half-full of water and about
¼ cup of coarse salt. Wait for it to boil. We use an outdoor cooker.
It's fast, and believe me, you don't want the smell of cooked
seafood in your home. When it starts to boil, throw in as many
lobsters, (with the elastics on their claws removed), as your pot
will hold. Get it boiling again, then cook for seventeen minutes.

You can have your lobster hot or cold; that is up to you. I like it both
ways. Don't forget to have some melted ADL butter handy to dip your
lobster meat into. This is a classic PEI meal that you will love. Enjoy!

INTERVIEW #17: Tara Anderson

(*Photo: supplied*)

Age at this writing: 40

Tara Anderson is a woman I know from our community. She is someone I can always have a conversation with. She's always struck me as a person who has designed her own life exactly how she's wanted. She is dedicated to her family and is proud of the career she's built for herself.

Q: What does the term 'farmwife' mean to you, and do you consider yourself to be one?"

A: "Yes for sure, I love being a farmwife! Being a farmwife for me is being present for my family. We work together as a team to help and support each other in all that we do! Jason is very passionate about all that he does to make our farm successful and I am there to encourage, listen, and help. At seeding and harvest I run meals out to the field, and help where I can with running men around. With three very active children, running my business from home, and taking care of our home and yard, I do find running the household to be my main focus at this stage of our life."

Q: Where do you live and how long have you lived there?

A: "We built our home seven miles southeast of Paradise Valley, Alberta, at my husband's family farm, and have lived here with our three children since July 2008. I have lived in the Paradise Valley area since I was five years old, aside from moving to Edmonton for a few years after high school to go to college and work."

Q: How long have you been married, and if you have children, how many do you have? Is this your first marriage?

A: "Nineteen years. Jason and I are high school sweethearts and were married in April 1997. We have had three children since."

Q: What was your background prior to marrying your husband?

A: "I was raised on an acreage north of Paradise Valley. After high school, I went on to Grant MacEwan Community College, where I was enrolled in the Travel Consulting program. I graduated and worked as a consultant for a year at Marlin Travel before getting married. We then moved back to Paradise Valley to start our life near Jason's family farm. I started as a travel consultant at Intra Royal Travel in Lloydminster (which changed to Carlson Wagonlit Travel while I was there), and worked there until we started our family two years later."

Q: Briefly describe your family farm business and its key players. If you have a business or career "off the farm," tell me about that, too.

A: "We have a mixed farming operation. We farm grain, cattle, and bison. Our daughters both ride and have horses to add to the mix. Caden, our youngest child, also started, and invested in his own chicken operation at the age of ten, raising 200 chickens on his own the first year. He has continued with this, and is always looking at options to improve what he is doing. There is never a dull moment around here!

I also work a business from home with a Swiss health and wellness company called Arbonne. I started this business ten years ago, in April, 2006. I never saw myself doing something like this but quickly realized that I had a lot of passion for the brand and believe in the products. It is about helping people. My favourite part about the business is teaching and training others alongside me! I help others by showing them how to live a life by design. We show people in Arbonne how to work a business around life, and when living on a farm, this is SO important! I think most moms feel torn between working and staying at home. This business allows them to have the best of both worlds: you can have a successful career all while being present with your kids and keeping your priorities straight! I love that there is no cap on how big you can build it; there really is no limit with this company! It truly is a gift and I love to share it with others."

Q: What do you consider your primary role?

A: "I would say that my primary role is being a wife and mom. My family is my priority for sure. I am also an entrepreneur and am blessed to be able to work with a company that allows me to keep my priorities straight."

Q: How do you ensure you are not sacrificing your "self" when farm life and work is so time-consuming?

A: "I have had to learn that I cannot do it all. I do my best and forget the rest. This does not come easily or naturally to me; I have to work on this daily. I like to do it all, and do it perfectly, but I have learned there is no such thing. I have had to delegate, and realize that in order for us to do all the things we each love to do, we all have to work together, and some jobs I have had to let go. I do take time to fill my own cup too, and learned years ago that if I am not taking care of myself I will have nothing to give the people I love. I have always made it a priority to work on myself personally by eating well, exercising, reading, and attending personal development training—and most importantly, placing God first in my life."

Q: Do you ever feel that being a farmwife takes away from any other personal goals you may have?

A: "I would not say it takes away from my goals, but it does sometimes make my journey to those goals longer then expected. Living on the farm during busy seasons, we have to be prepared to drop everything and go when needed to help. Jason has always been SUPER supportive of my dreams and goals in life too, so he would never want or wish me to compromise my goals for the farm. He gets it; he has dreams and desires too, and we help and encourage each other!"

Q: What is a key lesson we can learn from the older generations of farmwives?

A: "I remember listening to my Grandma Lorenz talk about being a farmwife. Hearing her stories, honestly I think the biggest thing I can learn from her is gratitude! She never complained, like EVER, but I know things were harder than she made them out to be because of her nature; I also know that I have A LOT to be thankful for! I cannot imagine having no running water or plumbing—the simple things we take for granted every day in our homes and on the farm."

Q: "What is a hilarious story you can learn about life on your farm?

A: "Okay this is funny now, but it wasn't at the time. It was seeding time, and Jason was working close to home seeding the crop. My sister was out visiting and we had just finished cooking supper, so we just had to run supper out to Jason in the field. My kids were still little, so we packed them all up into our van and headed out. I was going across the bin yard and saw "a little" water; I decided rather then go around it, I would just speed up. Well, epic fail. I am seriously dying laughing as I type this, remembering my sister's reaction. She was like, "You just drove into a slough!" The humbling part of this was having to call my husband, who was extremely busy trying to seed a crop (hence me trying to save him time by eating super in the field), to come and get us out. All I have to say is that I am glad my sister happened to be with me when he came to rescue me, because it caused a much milder reaction to my brilliant plan of attack. I think my husband was most shocked at the fact that I had not realized there is most often water in the spot I attempted to cross. Needless to say, he was not impressed, and less impressed still when he had to wade through the water and realize there really wasn't anything to hook a tow rope onto. Ah, that's what memories are made of, right?!"

Q: What are some ways you try to keep your marriage strong?

A: "Communication and making time for each other in the midst of our full life! Watching a friend of ours, with pretty much the exact same life as we have, lose her husband, I have realized that every day we get to spend together truly is a gift. I think being grateful for one another is so incredibly important in making the other person feel valued and appreciated. We also still date and (mush alert) he still makes my heart flutter!"

Q: For grain farmers, harvest is undoubtedly the busiest time of the year. How are harvest meals managed on your farm? (If you're not a grain farmer, pick an equally busy time of year on your farm and describe how meal times are managed.)

A: "The guys take out a lunch for the day and then we do supper in the field each night. My mother-in-law and myself typically alternate evenings to cook, so we are each only taking meals out every other night. It works great!"

Q: As you know, the demands of farming on your spouse's time is often such that they cannot contribute as much to home or childcare needs as spouses who work forty hours per week can. Describe how the never-ending task of housework is managed in your home.

A: "I am sure that most people can relate when I say that housework is a daily to-do in our home. After the kids leave for school, I usually spend time each day cleaning up and doing laundry. I actually don't really mind doing housework when I have time for it. As the kids have gotten busier, though, and more involved in activities I have found it more of a challenge to keep up with. The kids each help with daily chores, but we now pay our oldest daughter to do some weekly cleaning. She was looking for more ways to earn an income, and I needed the help, so we look at this as a win-win. She does not have to drive anywhere for the work, and it frees up time for myself what with running kids to sports / music activities, etc. and to work on my business."

Q: Having our families eat nutritious meals is becoming more and more a priority for families. Spending less time in the kitchen to achieve that, however, is also a necessity. What is a GREAT recipe your family can share that achieves both of these goals?

A: "Good nutrition is very important to me, and I work hard to make sure my family eats healthy! Because we are so on the go, I rely on my Crock-pot A LOT! Cabbage roll soup is a "go-to" for me because you just have to brown the meat, throw everything in the pot, and go!

CABBAGE ROLL SOUP

1 large onion
3 cloves of garlic, minced
1 lb. of lean ground beef
1/2 lb. of lean ground pork (or just use more beef)
3/4 cup uncooked long grain rice
1 medium head cabbage, chopped (core removed)
1 (28 oz.) can diced tomatoes
2 tbsp. tomato paste
4 cups beef broth
1 1/2 cups V8 or other vegetable juice

BILLI J MILLER

1 tsp. paprika
1 tsp. thyme
1 tbsp. Worcestershire sauce
1 bay leaf
salt and pepper to taste

In a large pot, brown the onion, garlic, pork, and beef. Drain any fat. Stir in the chopped cabbage and let cook until slightly softened (about 3 minutes). Add all remaining ingredients, bring to a boil, and reduce heat to medium low. Cover and simmer on low until rice is fully cooked (about 25–30 min). Remove bay leaf and serve.

For myself, after I brown the meat I literally throw it all in the Crock-pot and set on low for 8–10 hours. If you prefer a thinner soup you can add more beef broth; we just prefer it to be thicker and almost like a chili. I always tell my kids it was "made with love by mama too," which is where I get the eye rolls, lol.

Enjoy!

INTERVIEW #18: Samantha Cardinal

Age at this writing: 26

I met Samantha Cardinal at a book signing in St. Walburg, Saskatchewan, for my first book. She introduced herself and we began to talk. She lives on a farm just outside of Makwa, Saskatchewan, and has been there for almost four years. Her husband bought their farm in 2005, and they put a house on it in 2008. They've been married for two and a half years and have one daughter named Ashlynn.

Q: What does the term 'farmwife' mean to you, and do you consider yourself to be one?

A: "To me the term farmwife means 'keeper of the house.' The one who cooks and makes meals for the men in the field and then delivers it to the field. A farmwife keeps the house clean and the kids fed, clothed, and happy. A farmwife is a woman who can quickly pack up and go to the field to help out, or to pick up machinery and move fields while having dinner ready to go, whether for the field or when you come home. I am a farmwife and I wouldn't have it any other way."

Q: What was your background prior to marrying your husband?

A: "When I met Mike I worked for my parents at Tru Hardware in St. Walburg, Saskatchewan. I continued to work there while helping Mike out on the farm. After I had Ashlynn, we decided that me being a stay-at-home mom would be the best decision."

Q: Briefly describe your family farm business and its key players. If you have a business or career "off the farm," tell me about that, too.

A: "We are grain farmers. We grow peas, wheat, canola, and forage to some ranchers. This is the second year that we can stay home in the winters as full-time farmers."

Q: What do you think the primary difference is between the younger generations of farmwives and the women that came before them?

A: "I think the main difference between the two generations is technology. Without cell phones I know it would be a lot harder to find out exactly where my husband is in the field to pick him up, or drop off supper. Manual labour is lessened, but farming now is on a much larger scale. Manual labour has been reduced due to larger equipment and newer and more efficient ways of farming."

Q: How do you think this may differ from the generations before you?

A: "I think the farmwives, my mother-in-law in particular, had a lot more responsibility. My in-laws have been farming for forty-five years and they went through many hardships. Now they are able to help us out with wisdom and guidance."

Q: What is the best part of life on a farm for you?

A: "My favourite part of life on the farm is the peace and quiet. I love being out in the middle of nowhere. Whether there is three feet of snow on the ground or it's the heart of summer, every day is great on the farm."

Q: How do you ensure you are not sacrificing your "self" when farm life and work is so time-consuming?

A: "I usually like to take some time at the end of the day and just relax and think about the day. A hot shower and a good show after the baby goes to bed is a good way to relax and unwind."

Q: Do you ever feel that being a farmwife takes away from any other personal goals you may have?

A: "Being a mom, raising our family, and helping my husband farm are my goals. Spending as much time as we can together is priority, whether it be on a combine ride, crop checking, a trip to town to go get fertilizer, or those rainy days where you can't turn a wheel. Our lives are the farm and I couldn't be happier with how my life has turned out."

Q: What is a key lesson we can learn from the older generations of farmwives?

A: "My mother-in-law, Margaret, has taught me a few key lessons, including:
1. Always cook lots of food. It's better to have leftovers than hungry men.
2. Money isn't everything. As long as we have our health and we are all still together, that is all that matters."

Q: What is a hilarious story you can learn about life on your farm?

A: "Well there are a few, but this is one tops the list for me. The first time I went for a combine ride with Mike, I took the biggest blanket I could find, a winter jacket, a toque, and mitts; I was expecting it to be cold. Let's just say that I learned that combines have good heaters. We laughed for a long time after that."

Q: What do you consider the biggest challenge for women entering into / living life on the farm?

A: "I would say the biggest challenge for me is spending lots of time alone when my husband is farming. Once seeding is underway and things get busy on the farm, crop checking, taking meals to the fix, and having quick little visits are nice—you have to take what time you have together when you can."

Q: What's the most important thing you hope your children learn from farm life?

A: "I want my children to learn good work ethic. To always be willing to lend a helping hand. I want my children to know that farming is more than just a job, it's a way of life, and there are so many opportunities on the farm."

Q: What are some ways you try to keep your marriage strong?

A: "Never go to bed angry. Communication is key. Always support and encourage each other."

Q: When it all just seems too much (life, responsibilities, the juggling act) what is something you do for self-care?

A: "Talk / vent with my husband, a long hot shower, and a nice cup of tea."

Q: For grain farmers, harvest is undoubtedly the busiest time of the year. How are harvest meals managed on your farm? (If you're not a grain farmer, pick an equally busy time of year on your farm and describe how meal times are managed.)

A: "I make lunch for my husband the night before (usually sandwiches or leftovers) and I make supper and deliver it to the field. If we are helping Mike's parents harvest or vice versa, I like to make supper and let my mother-in-law help take semis to the field, run the men to different fields, test grain, or whatever they need her to do."

Q: Having our families eat nutritious meals is becoming more and more a priority for families. Spending less time in the kitchen to achieve that, however, is also a necessity. What is a GREAT recipe your family can share that achieves both of these goals?

A: "I have a couple of recipes that are a huge hit in my kitchen. Both of the following are tried, tested, and true. One recipe comes from my mother's kitchen and the other from my mother-in-law's kitchen."

LASAGNE (MY MOM'S RECIPE)

Lasagne noodles
1 lb. hamburger meat
1 jar spaghetti sauce
500 ml. cottage cheese
Fresh or frozen spinach
1 egg
Mozzarella and marble cheese, grated

Spread a bit of sauce on the bottom of the pan. Cook the lasagne noodles, then rinse in cold water. Brown the hamburger meat and add sauce. In a separate bowl combine the cottage cheese, spinach, egg, and grated cheese. Layer 3 lasagne noodles in the pan, then spread the hamburger mixture, then another layer of noodles, followed by the cottage cheese mixture and alternate. For the final layer, place 3 lasagne noodles and top with cheese. Cover with foil and bake at 325 degrees for 40–60 minutes.

BILLI J MILLER
UNBAKED GRAHAM WAFER SQUARE (MY MOTHER-IN-LAW'S RECIPE)

1 egg, beaten
1/2 cup margarine
1 cup brown sugar
1/3 cup milk
1 cup Graham wafers, finely chopped

Bring mixture to a boil. Stir occasionally and let bubble for
2–3 minutes. Remove from heat and add Graham wafers.

Mix in:

1 cup coconut
1/2 tsp. vanilla

Line the bottom of an 8 x 11" pan with additional Graham
wafers. Pour in the mixture and layer whole wafers over the
top. Chill in the fridge then spread butter icing over this.

Icing:

4 tbsp. butter
2 cups icing sugar
1/2 tsp. vanilla
3 tbsp. milk or cream

INTERVIEW #19: Amy Hill

(*Photo: supplied*)

Age at this writing: 31

Amy Hill hails from Cooks Brook, Nova Scotia. She lives on a farm that she and her husband started from the ground up in 2011.

Q: What does the term 'farmwife' mean to you, and do you consider yourself to be one?"

A: "The term farmwife always held negative connotations to me growing up. I looked at the term to mean someone who serves their husband meals and cleans the house and raises the children, but who has no other role on the farm. I wanted more. I know the term can mean just that (which is fantastic for those who wish to be in that role), but it can also mean so many more things. I am a farmwife in that I am a wife and I am a farmer. I do the traditional roles that one may associate with a farmwife as I cook all of our meals from scratch, mainly from items we grow on property; I clean the home and take care of our daughter; and I also run all parts of the farm. I want my daughter to grow up knowing that she can be both a caregiver to her family as well as a boss in business."

Q: What was your background prior to marrying your husband?

A: "I have my B.Sc. Ag. in Animal Sciences. I worked for five years in wildlife rehabilitation and then started my farm in early 2011 while living on a dairy farm that my husband (then partner) worked on."

Q: Briefly describe your family farm business and its key players. If you have a business or career "off the farm," tell me about that, too.

A: "Our farm was started from the ground up in 2011 when my husband and I decided that we wanted a farm of our own (he had always worked on dairy farms). We wanted to raise our animals on pasture, feed them non-GMO grains, and help to decrease waste by also using discarded produce from our local grocers as feed. We also wanted to grow vegetables organically and figured they would tie into our system well. My husband switched to carpentry to pay the bills while I started the farm and that is where we still are today. Currently we sell our meat from farm and in select stores across Nova Scotia and our produce is available alongside our eggs and meat in our Community Supported Agriculture (CSA) Program. I run all aspects of the farm, from garden planning, planting, harvesting, hauling feed and water, breeding, cleaning, and moving livestock to sales, website design and upkeep, social media, taxes, and deliveries. I do the daily run of the farm, with my three-year-old daughter at my side, while my husband works in the city. He is often found fixing things around the farm or helping me with trailering our livestock during the evenings and weekends, and spends any extra time that he has helping me out with larger tasks. We also welcome volunteers through the WWOOF program to our farm, where they live with us for a period of time in exchange for their help.

In my spare time, or I guess when I squeeze it in and can find someone to cover the farm chores for me, I am a birth doula. Since having my daughter I have had this passion to help women become more educated in their options regarding labour, birth, and postpartum. I want women to know the strength that their bodies are capable of and help them to truly take a hold of their births. It would be a dream to be able to tie in my love for birth and more midwife-centred delivery with my farm. Maybe one day I'll have something similar to Ina May's farm in the States—a girl can dream!"

Q: What do you consider your primary role?

A: "I do not have a primary role. I feel that my farm was my first child, born from love and passion for the land, from both my husband and I, and now my daughter is part of this too. I often dream of a day when I can maybe have someone come in and handle a smaller part of the farm, perhaps the social media, so that I can focus on other areas, but I honestly like to be involved with every aspect, so I may have a hard time letting go."

Q: What is your husband's role in your family and on the farm?

A: "My husband often works long hours off-farm but his carpentry work is extremely important to our success. He has fully renovated our large barn to include wash stations and heated plant rooms; he builds livestock fences and shelters as well as baby barns. He is also a father to our daughter which, for us, means we split all night wakings, diaper changes, kissing 'ouchies,' and games of tag or hide-and-go-seek."

Q: What is the best part of life on a farm for you?

A: "My favourite part of farm life is getting to see how our food gets to our plate after starting from only an idea. My daughter can help me to plan out a garden or a breeding pair and within the year we have full meals nourishing our bodies and helping us to grow: a direct result of our hard work."

Q: Has there been anything in your family or farm life that you've wanted to change?

A: "I would love to be successful enough with the farm to bring my husband on property with us. While I love being a strong, independent business owner, I also know that the growth of the farm means I need extra help to accomplish everything and I would most like that role to be my partner in life's. Since farming is a lifestyle and not just a job it makes the most sense to bring him into this full time."

Q: "What is a hilarious story you can learn about life on your farm?

A: "Farming primarily by myself I have been left in many situations that I can laugh at now. One of the funniest was when I was around six or seven months pregnant with my daughter. I had set up a 10' x 30' green-house and anchored it down with what I had thought were sufficient enough posts. We had a windy day and my entire greenhouse lifted into the air and started blowing down the field. I grabbed onto it and it was lifting me off the ground as it sailed through the pastures. With one hand I called my neighbour and asked him to come and help. I know it must have looked crazy seeing a 5'3" pregnant woman fighting with this giant kite of a greenhouse, but he was fast at getting down to me and helping me repair the damage."

Q: What do you consider the biggest challenge for women entering into / living life on the farm?

A: "I think that many of us want to be caregivers and do it all. We spend so much time looking after others that we often neglect ourselves and after time it gets hard to fill others cups when your own is empty."

Q: What are some ways you try to keep your marriage strong?

A: "Communication. We don't have a television in our home and I feel that it has really helped to keep our lines of communication open with each other. We sit down in the evenings and we talk, we ask questions, we care. This doesn't mean that we never get tired and frustrated and close up for a bit but we make sure to always come back to each other and discuss it all, because this life is hard and you need a strong foundation of trust and communication to get through it."

Q: For grain farmers, harvest is undoubtedly the busiest time of the year. How are harvest meals managed on your farm? (If you're not a grain farmer, pick an equally busy time of year on your farm and describe how meal times are managed.)

A: "Our farm is pretty much always busy but late spring / early summer is when we have a full farmload. Food takes a high priority in our home as we cannot farm if we do not fuel ourselves! I have gotten rather good at planning out meals for days when I know I will be full tilt, and often cook meals that could feed ten people at a time so there are always plenty of leftovers."

Q: When it all just seems too much (life, responsibilities, the juggling act) what is something you do for self-care?

A: "I'm still trying to figure that one out. I have to say it's a major weak point in my life and I often get completely drained before finally deciding to take a break."

Q: Having our families eat nutritious meals is becoming more and more a priority for families. Spending less time in the kitchen to achieve that, however, is also a necessity. What is a GREAT recipe your family can share that achieves both of these goals?

A: "To be honest, most of the meals that I cook are made completely from scratch, bread and all, which tends to take time, but we do love to have tomato soup with warm sweet rolls on cold evenings. I don't work with exact recipes but this is approximately how we make the tomato soup."

TOMATO SOUP & SWEET ROLLS

Soup:

4–5 lbs. tomatoes
4 cups of chicken broth
1 onion, chopped
4 cloves garlic, minced

Bring all of these to a boil and then reduce to medium and simmer for 30 minutes. Blend together and then strain if skins were left on tomatoes. Make a roux in a shallow pot and slowly pour in the tomato mixture. Add cream if you like it creamier.

Soft, sweet rolls:

2 tbsp. yeast
1 cup hot water
4 tbsp. melted coconut oil
3 tbsp. honey
1 egg
1 tsp. salt
3 1/2 cups flour

Preheat the oven to 425 degrees. Dissolve the yeast in hot water in a mixing bowl and then stir in the oil and honey. Let the yeast activate for approximately 5 minutes. Add the egg, salt, and 2 ½ cups of flour and begin to knead. Continue adding flour until it forms a soft dough. Knead on a floured surface until smooth and elastic. Immediately cut into 12 equal pieces and shape into balls. Place on a greased pan (I use cast iron), cover, and rest for 15 minutes. Bake for 8–12 minutes until golden brown on the surface.

INTERVIEW #20: Melissa Wright

(*Photo credit: Sonéy Delport* (SD Imaging))

Age at this writing: 42

Melissa lives on a family farm/ranch near Rivercourse, Alberta. She's been there since 2002 when she married her husband Derek. They have four children together: Holly (12), Hannah (10), Hayden (8), and Hope (6). Melissa's husband Derek has known my husband since Kindergarten and now our kids go to the same school also. Melissa is successful in her career and is an active member of her community. They are a family that lives their life with passion for what they do and hard work.

Q: What does the term 'farmwife' mean to you, and do you consider yourself to be one?

A: "I absolutely consider myself to be a farmwife. It means sharing in the highs and lows of a volatile industry and being there to support one another. It is sharing a lifestyle that I truly value."

Q: What was your background prior to marrying your husband?

A: "I had a fantastic childhood growing up on a ranch north of Lloydminster with my parents and two older brothers. My uncle Frank and his family were close by. As a little girl I dreamed of becoming a nurse (like my mom), marrying a rancher, and having children.

Prior to marrying Derek I had spent the previous four winters as a travel nurse in the United States, returning home to my parents' ranch for the summer. I valued working with my parents and brothers on the ranch and running my own herd of yearling steers. Beyond a doubt my favourite activity is moving cattle by horseback. Any major cattle moves, when possible, were scheduled on days I was not nursing at the Lloydminster Hospital or Doctor Cooke Extended Care.

In 2001, with my Gram aging and the opportunity to work for Grant MacEwan College (in Edmonton, Alberta) as Rural Nursing Instructor, I decided to quit travel nursing. At that time I had been dating Derek for two years, so it was definitely time to stay home and see where the relationship was going."

Q: Briefly describe your family farm business and its key players. If you have a business or career "off the farm," tell me about that, too.

A: "Today Derek, his parents Keith and Marilyn, and myself work together on a cattle / grain farm. Derek's company is completely separate from his parents' and Derek and I keep our business affairs completely separate. My mom to this day operates a separate cattle company from my dad, which has influenced me to maintain this same level of autonomy within my farming / ranching relationship with Derek. I have a small herd of cows, continue to run a yearling steer program, and have a few acres of cropland. With that said, Derek does the majority of work unless the job at hand requires me being on the back of a horse. In that case, the work is scheduled around my nursing shifts.

Presently I work part-time as Clinical Nurse Educator with Prairie North Health Region and as a casual staff nurse in the Lloydminster Hospital ER. I also do contract work for the University of Saskatchewan as a clinical instructor or faculty resource while students complete clinical rotations within the health region."

Q: What do you consider your primary role?

A: "During harvest, my mother-in-law drives a combine so I take on the role of making and delivering the supper meal to the field. Before we had children I did some land rolling and baling, but to be truly honest my passions outside of my family are nursing, working with cattle, and riding horses. Long hours on farm equipment is not my thing. I do enjoy helping with the work related to the cow / calf part of the operation. I feel my off-farm income contributes by enabling Derek to put a greater portion of his profits back into growing the farm."

Q: What is your husband's role in your family and on the farm?

A: "Derek is the sole decision maker when it comes to running his farm / ranch. I really struggle with the cost of equipment and inputs. I have come to trust that he is making the best business decisions. With that said, I do appreciate being somewhat informed on the arrival of a new piece of equipment and not finding out by overhearing my father-in-law at the local hockey rink, or answering a call from the machinery dealer who is wondering if Derek will be around to sign the papers on his new piece of equipment!

When it comes to my portion of the farm, as stated earlier, he does most of the work. He always consults with me with regard to when I want to sell grain or cattle, but I leave the input and marketing decisions to him."

Q: Have you started any new traditions in your family that are important to you?

A: "The only thing that comes to mind is that growing up in my family everyone was capable and willing to prepare and clean up supper. While this is an ongoing area of implementation, Derek has become pretty accepting of the tradition."

Q: On some Canadian farms where multiple families are involved, there are a variety of land- and home-ownership complexities that still exist today. In terms of the ownership setup of your farm, is there anything that worries you about your own or your children's security?

A: "I worry about the loss of my husband. I would have no idea how to manage the farm, nor would there be the margin to hire all the labour out. I would want to keep the farm going so my children can be raised with the lifestyle that it provides and so there would be the option for one of them to take it over."

Q: Has there been anything you were not prepared for since becoming a farmwife?

A: "Yes, I had no idea how expensive crop input and equipment costs were. In 2002, the year we married, the drought was so bad we didn't combine an acre. The next year we were hit with BSE, which caused the cattle market to crash. Derek was continuing to try to expand his operation and I really could not see how we were going to make a go of it. I was starting to think he should 'throw the towel in' and get a trucking job. I am so grateful that he has been able to develop the farm / ranch to where it is today, because there is no greater lifestyle."

Q: "What is a key lesson we can learn from the older generations of farmwives?

A: "This question makes me think of the two most important older generation farmwives in my life. My Gram, Holly Wells, while she was not one to give advice, would want me to support Derek 100 percent and not question his decisions. My mom's advice is to keep my farm / ranch separate from Derek's. This advice is what has helped me accept the parts of farming that I was not prepared for and protect my independence."

Q: "What is a hilarious story you can share about life on your farm?

A: "The second summer we were married I was anxious to help with the baling. The baler at that time took forty seconds to tie a bale, which was way too long for me to sit idol, so I chose to read a paragraph of a book each time. Well, this led to a few broken bales left in the field for the cows to clean up. Consequently, since then, the rest of the family has not been too quick to suggest that I operate a piece of farm equipment."

Q: Do you have an app or "hack" to keep yourself organized that you cannot live without?

A: "My favourite "app" is podcasts. When you have long hours in the kitchen preparing supper, packing it in coolers and unpacking and doing dishes, listening to a good podcast is a game changer. When tidying the house, I stay inspired by listening to a de-cluttering / organizing podcast."

Q: Is there any piece of advice you wish you had received when beginning your life as a farmwife, and what advice would you give to women marrying into farm life today?

A: "When we were first married, we joined the McLaughlin Hall. When you work in a different community and do not have children, it can be hard to become involved and get to know the community. While we have become too busy with our kids' activities to continue our membership, joining the hall was a great way to meet neighbours. One evening while visiting after a meeting, the topic turned to holidays and Vickie Elliott shared the benefits of the TD Infinite Travel Visa card. I applied for one of those cards. While farming may have a limited margin for extra spending, the use of a good points card has enabled us to take some very memorable family holidays. Outside of getting a good travel points Visa card I have no advice to share, because, as they say, "there is more than one way to skin a cat." Do what works for your relationship and your farming situation because no two family farms operate the same."

Q: For grain farmers, harvest is undoubtedly the busiest time of the year. How are harvest meals managed on your farm? (If you're not a grain farmer, pick an equally busy time of year on your farm and describe how meal times are managed.)

A: "Everyone takes their own bagged lunch and I am in charge of the supper meal. Including our kids and myself, there is a group of twelve to enjoy a meal in the field most evenings. On cooler evenings, or if the kids have activities, I will send the coolers to the field. Prior to harvest I try to have my deep freezers full of desserts and meals to dump in the slow-cooker or place in the oven with the timer on. Between having our own beef and fresh garden produce at that time of year, I do not find there is a significant change to our grocery bill. My mom donates produce that grows much better in her garden, as well as an ample selection of preserves that enhance the meals."

Q: As you know, the demands of farming on your spouse's time is often such that they cannot contribute as much to home or childcare needs as spouses who work forty hours per week can. Describe how the never-ending task of housework is managed in your home.

A: "Yes, Derek would average way more than a forty-hour workweek, but I feel that farming / ranching has flexibility (outside of harvest and seeding) that has contributed to him providing more childcare than a person with an off-farm job might. I start work at 7 am, so he is in charge of getting the kids on the bus most mornings. I do adjust my schedule to work less during seeding and harvest. After working on the farm all day, Derek looks forward to taking the kids to extracurricular activities in the evening. I look forward to staying home and organizing the kids' / household activities on that end. When the kids were pre-school age they went with Derek for all farming activities that it was safe for them to attend. We have been very fortunate to have help from his mom on an as-needed basis.

I have found laundry to be very overwhelming. I do try to be constantly washing and stacking clean baskets in my laundry room. A couple times a week I will dump it all on the couch and enjoy a movie or Dr. Oz while I fold. As for the house, it can get out of hand but we are continuing to become more organized and have less clutter. Last fall we built a mudroom in our garage and each person has their own stall. This area includes large shelves for hockey equipment. The biggest help is having a lady come clean every two weeks. No matter how tired we are the night before she comes, the house has to be 'de-cluttered!'

I try to stay on top of meals by having something in the slow-cooker or the oven when I am going to be away for the day or outside working. We have two deep freezers full of food and an overstocked cold storage room. I aim to only shop for groceries twice a month. With that said, Derek does get frustrated with making lunches from time to time and will stop at the Co-op and buy a whole bunch of 'crap' that I would never put in the cart."

Q: Having our families eat nutritious meals is becoming more and more a priority for families. Spending less time in the kitchen to achieve that, however, is also a necessity. What is a GREAT recipe your family can share that achieves both of these goals?

A: "I make meatballs and hamburgers up in 12-lb. batches. The meatballs are very handy to place in the slow-cooker in the morning. The older girls are now to the age they can put rice and vegetables on and make a salad to go with it."

MAKE-AHEAD HAMBURGERS OR MEATBALLS

12 lbs. ground beef
1 can evaporated milk
2 cups fine breadcrumbs
3 tbsp. Worcestershire sauce
1 tbsp. pepper
3 tbsp. seasoning salt
1/2 tbsp. garlic powder

Mix above ingredients together. For hamburgers, take fist-sized balls and flatten to ½ inch width between wax paper. Stack in piles and freeze. For meatballs, roll into 1-inch balls and cook on a bar pan (stoneware works well) at 400 degrees until brown. Place meatballs in rows in a large freezer bag. Freeze hamburgers and meatballs for quick meals.

SLOW-COOKER SWEET AND SOUR MEATBALLS

If using fresh meatballs, brown in the oven before placing in slow-cooker; if frozen, drop directly into slow-cooker.

Sauce:

3/4 cup brown sugar
1/3 cup vinegar
1/2 cup ketchup
1/2 cup water
1 tsp. dried mustard
1 can crushed pineapple (optional)

Mix and pour over meatballs and cook on high for 3–4 hours or low for 8–10.

INTERVIEW #21: Karen Lester

(*Photo: supplied*)

Age at this writing: 40

Karen and Nancy, the women in the following two interviews, come from St. John's, Newfoundland. They both live on the Lester family farm that has been operating for over 160 years. It now consists of a dairy operation and a vegetable production operation. Karen is married to Chris Lester, who runs the field operations of the vegetable production along with his brother Brad. Karen and Chris met in high school, married in 2001, and have one child. They were both born in St. John's.

Q: What does the term 'farmwife' mean to you, and do you consider yourself to be one?

A: "I'm the wife of a farmer, which I guess gives me the title of farmwife. I however don't see the term as a role. I don't see my role as a partner as any different than any other partner of an entrepreneur. When you own your own business, you never actually leave it. It is part of who you are and oftentimes you have to respond outside "regular" hours. In Newfoundland in particular, my husband has to go out overnight to ensure plants are protected from frost, greenhouses are safe from wind, and animals are secure and where they should be. As the phrase goes, "the cows don't know it's Sunday.""

Q: Briefly describe your family farm business and its key players. If you have a business or career "off the farm," tell me about that, too.

A: "The Lester family has been farming in St. John's for over 160 years. The current version of the farm is split between two brothers. Colin Lester and his family manage the dairy operation and John Lester and his family run the vegetable production. John is my father-in-law. Lester's Farm Market has evolved over the years from a wholesale vegetable operation to a direct market store. In 1994, my mother-in-law, Mary, felt that selling wholesale meant that the farm couldn't control the product getting to the customer. She decided to remove the middleman and literally hauled a table to the side of the road to sell vegetables. Today, the building sells our own vegetables, beef, eggs, honey, and more. We have a petting barn, full flower greenhouses, we cater to school tours, and have over 400 children enrolled in our 'Lil Lesters' program. This program is led by my sister-in-law, Susan, who has a degree in Education and English. This program runs throughout the summer and gives kids a sense of farming with experiential learning. My husband, Chris, and his brother, Brad, run the field operations where they grow everything from asparagus to zucchini.

I went to Memorial University and received my Bachelor of Commerce. I currently work at the university in a management role. I've held roles in marketing and project management."

Q: What do you consider your primary role?

A: "I feel my role is to support Chris. My view on this, however, is not to blindly follow and agree with everything he says. The farm has changed throughout the years. When the farm operated through wholesale, there was harvest and sale. Simple. Now there are staff, customers, social media, media relations, public presentations, government relations, and farm boards. With my marketing background, I help where I can in these aspects."

Q: What is your husband's role in your family and on the farm?

A: "Since our daughter is only six months old and we haven't been through an entire season yet, we are still navigating the waters of what our roles will be as new parents. We've done quite well to date; we have and honest relationship where we talk about who is doing what. This is also very fluid. As I type this, he's doing dishes. I made supper. He put our daughter to bed tonight while I worked out and I put her to bed last night. I feel our family may look a little different than it may have years ago. I think it is important that we both take an active role in developing our daughter. Also, where our farm is very seasonal in Newfoundland, our roles change in the winter, when oftentimes Chris is home from work before I am. The key is to communicate about what needs to be done and who's doing it."

Q: Has there been anything in your family or farm life that you've wanted to change?

A: "Of course! Farming isn't a job; it's in your blood. You don't leave at 5 pm, lock your office and worry about what isn't done tomorrow. You don't fill out a form to ask your boss for two weeks off for a family vacation. There are times I wish it could be left behind. I've had suppers at my in-laws' before that seem more like a farm meeting. I understand that this is their only time to talk and it is productive; however, if I'm being honest, I'd love more time talking about things other than the farm."

Q: On some Canadian farms where multiple families are involved, there are a variety of land- and home-ownership complexities that still exist today. In terms of the ownership setup of your farm, is there anything that worries you about your own or your children's security?

A: "In Newfoundland, we have an agricultural freeze on land. This means that the government owns much of the farmland in the province and the farmers lease this land long-term. So much of our own land isn't technically ours. Also, it is difficult to use farmland for residential use. The amount of paperwork is extraordinary when it comes to building a home on farmland. I would personally like to see this change for those family members that decide to take jobs on the farm. Farming is a selfless commitment that is grossly underpaid. I'd hate to work out my husband's hourly wage. So I feel that those who commit to the farm should benefit from other perks where possible. This would include land acquisition."

Q: "What is a hilarious story you can learn about life on your farm?

A: "Cows don't know it's Sunday and emus can't tell time. One night I got a call from my mother-in-law at 4:30 am. On the other end of the phone she says, "Is Chris there? The emus are out." Thinking it was some sort of prank, I reluctantly told Chris and he left for the farm. When he got down there, his sister, mother, and father are all out looking for two emus that had gotten out. One had crossed the road, so my mother-in-law was in the middle of the road ensuring they didn't cross again and get hit by a car. At this moment, a police car drives by and stops to see if she is okay. She asks the officer "Have you seen a big bird?" Clearly questioning her sanity (it's 4:30 am and she's looking for a big bird), the officer responds, "Have YOU seen a big bird?" She quickly assures she's with the farm and the emus have been let out. The emus were eventually caught and returned. Not before they clawed my father-in-law's wool sweater to shreds."

Q: What are you most proud of in life?

A: "My husband and I struggled with fertility for many years—over ten years and multiple fertility treatments—we couldn't make anything work. In 2016, my sister carried Eva for us. I am proud that I stayed strong and didn't give up. I'm also proud that Chris and I are stronger from the experience. To say that this was a challenging time would be an understatement. There were legal contracts, therapy sessions, medical appointments, and expensive trips to Ottawa, where we had the treatment. This can be too much for some couples; however, Chris and I saw this as a team effort and became even closer through this process. The outcome is our beautiful daughter, who was born in December 2016."

Q: For grain farmers, harvest is undoubtedly the busiest time of the year. How are harvest meals managed on your farm? (If you're not a grain farmer, pick an equally busy time of year on your farm and describe how meal times are managed.)

A: "When our farm is in full harvest, and around our annual Pumpkin Fest is probably our busiest time of year. Meals at that time are not easy, as some nights have gone quite late. We use our slow-cooker a lot. It is a great way for us both to have a hot meal at different times. Between chili and roasts, it's great and easy! Also, it's great to freeze these meals and have on hand. Before I started maternity leave I froze several meals and it's great to have some on hand on days there is less time available."

Q: As you know, the demands of farming on your spouse's time is often such that they cannot contribute as much to home or childcare needs as spouses who work forty hours per week can. Describe how the never-ending task of housework is managed in your home.

A: "It really is a team effort. We know the chores that we like to do and who is better at them. I do the majority of the cooking and Chris does the dishes. He sweeps, I mop. We each do our own laundry. During the busy times on the farm, I step up and do a little more, and during the winter when he is home, vice versa. The key is really to ensure communication and that there are no assumptions about who is doing what."

Q: When it all just seems too much (life, responsibilities, the juggling act) what is something you do for self-care?

A: "Twice a week, myself and Chris' cousin, Nancy, go to a local boxing place called "BoxFit" for a boxercise class. It is a high-energy class with great music and amazing women. It's a nice chance to do something for myself, laugh a little, and burn some calories. It also gives Chris some "daddy / daughter time." We both look forward to it."

Q: Having our families eat nutritious meals is becoming more and more a priority for families. Spending less time in the kitchen to achieve that, however, is also a necessity. What is a GREAT recipe your family can share that achieves both of these goals?

CHILI

For me, chili is so easy to do in a slow-cooker and freezes great for future meals. Cook up some ground beef and add that to the slow-cooker, then add vegetables that you might like. Our preference is onions, corn, and peppers. Add in some chili seasoning, kidney beans, hot sauce, and tomato sauce. 4–6 hours in the slow-cooker and supper is ready. I've also done this recipe with leftover chicken or turkey as well.

(*Photo: supplied*)

Age at this writing: 34

Nancy Lester-Rideout was born and raised in St. John's, Newfoundland. Her Father, Colin, heads up the Dairy operation at Lester Farms alongside his wife, Trish, son Craig, and Nancy. Nancy met her husband Chris in 2006, and they have been married since November 2013. They have one boy, born in 2014.

Q: What does the term 'farmwife' mean to you, and do you consider yourself to be one?

A: "To me, a farmwife, is a woman that keeps the household going. Someone that keeps the house clean, prepares ALL meals, watches the children, and doesn't have time to do much out around the farm.

I'm not gonna lie, I struggled with this question. Because I don't really consider myself a "farmwife. Mostly because I consider myself a dairy farmer first? (if that makes any sense to you!) I do however, keep the house clean (on most days lol) I do spend more time with our little boy Ryan, but I think Chris (my husband) actually prepares more meals. He can do a great BBQ, or what we Newfoundlanders call"Jiggs Dinner" but my skills are more along the lines of kraft dinner and chicken nuggets. Haha. Also, Ryan is in a day home during the week, so I'm out around the farm while he's there. That's why I consider the term "farmwife" to be a tricky one. Don't tell Chris, but maybe he's the "farmhusband!!! hahahaha I joke with him about that."

Q: What was your background prior to marrying your husband?

A: "After graduating from high school, I attended Memorial University for three years, but soon learned that the farm was where I wanted to be. Before Chris and I were married, I worked full time (meaning farm full time—sixty plus hours a week, haha) at Lester's Dairy Farm. At the time we milked 280 cows twice a day. Before I met Chris I actually worked at Lester's Farm Market, which my aunt, uncle, and cousins own. I always loved interacting with people and the atmosphere, however, shortly after meeting Chris I made the decision to work full time on our family dairy farm, alongside my mom, dad, and brother."

Q: Briefly describe your family farm business and its key players. If you have a business or career "off the farm," tell me about that, too.

A: "I look after the overall herd health, weekly veterinarian check-ups, milking, caring for baby calves, cleaning and maintaining the milking equipment, keeping the place tidy, doing the schedule for our six employees, and any school or group tours that come up.

My brother Craig looks after the management of cow nutrition, fertility, and genetics, as well as most fieldwork, including manure spreading, mowing hay, hay harvesting, hay storage, spraying fields, snow clearing and so on. Also any farm improvements and future growth, along with any applications that need to be completed.

My dad Colin is scaling back from being in the barn as much but he still loves to look after feeding the cows every day when he's around. He also does all land clearing, snow clearing, and he transports any feed, fertilizer, hay, or whatever we may need from neighbouring provinces. Dad also helps with any applications that need to be completed as well.

My mom Trish feeds all of us every day, (lunch times are catch up times, where we can chat about what we all have planned for the future of our farm hourly, daily, and yearly). God knows that working with family can be quite the challenge sometimes, so mom lends an ear to anyone that needs to talk about whatever. She does all the book work and payroll, comes out on the farm when she's needed (this past year, we needed help putting tires on our silage pile to keep the plastic down before the wind came up, and dad called to asked her to help out, and she sure did!). She really is the glue that holds us all together.

My husband Chris is a certified heavy equipment operator, so he can do all tractor work, including manure spreading, hay harvest, land clearing, and he has great mechanic skills so he helps maintain and fix all equipment as well. When we first met, he would come in the barn just to help out when I was milking, but that doesn't happen so much anymore now that were married!"

Q: What do you consider your primary role?

A: "Right now, my primary role is to be a great mom for our little boy, Ryan. I'm very fortunate that on my family farm I can work my schedule around my son. Since Ryan was born, we switched to milking three times a day (5 am, 1 pm, and 9 pm), which actually works out great, because it gives me the time to check on any cows that need more attention in the morning, along with keeping all our cow info in our computers up-to-date, and then at 1 pm I can do the milking and be finished to pick up my son from the day home. And on days when things go wrong (which we all know happens often) I can ask my mom to pick up Ryan."

Q: What is your husband's role in your family and on the farm?

A: "In terms of family, to be a great role model for Ryan, and to be a great husband to me! He loves to teach Ryan about his love for hunting, and even about tractors, which he likes best. Out on the farm, see question 4. Before I met Chris, my brother would always joke that whoever I dated had to be useful on the farm! Haha, I think I did pretty good, and Craig would agree! "

Q: Has there been anything in your family or farm life that you've wanted to change?

A: "I've actually already had to change my farm life since Ryan was born. Before Ryan, I worked 5–6 days a week, starting my day at 4:30 am, and we would all take turns working the holidays. But now with Ryan I take him to his day home for 8 am and work all day until he gets picked up at 4:30. I'm very fortunate that I'm able to take the time to do this. (Sometimes I don't have time to shower before I get Ryan, and every time he says "Mom, you stinky?" Haha.)"

Q: On some Canadian farms where multiple families are involved, there are a variety of land- and home-ownership complexities that still exist today. In terms of the ownership setup of your farm, is there anything that worries you about your own or your children's security?

A: "There's always going to be that worry. And being right in the middle of the city, there's always that worry that we may be forced to move on. However, there is an agricultural freeze on the land, which we are very grateful for, so that gives us some peace of mind. I'd like to mention, too, that we are very lucky that our government is very supportive of the agriculture industry, both provincially and federally, so that is a great help as well."

I do have an older sister, Jill, who worked on our farm when she was younger, but she chose another career. Jill, Craig, and I have a good relationship, and Jill has often told us that she understands that because she chose to leave our family farm (due to the 365 workdays, early mornings, late evenings, and no civic holidays), that she doesn't expect anything from the farm. Don't get me wrong, Jill is still a workaholic and puts 110 percent into her career. We are very lucky that Jill has this attitude because I have heard of cases of off-farm family members thinking differently."

Q: What is a hilarious story you can learn about life on your farm?

A: "Years ago, we used to use a bull for breeding (now it's all done artificially) and EVERY SINGLE TIME we would have a school tour come through, the bull would end up breeding a cow while I was trying to be serious and educate the kids! I would usually just tell them that he was getting a "piggy back ride" and guide the kids to another area!"

Q: What is the most important thing you hope your children learn from farm life?

A: "I hope Ryan learns to respect the animals and the land. Cows are amazing, hard working creatures, and they deserve respect, 100 percent. Also the land. Because we are in the city, we deal a lot with issues regarding ATVs tearing up our fields. Newfoundland is called "The Rock" for a reason. It takes generations of rock removal to get the fields ready to grow our crop, and it upsets us when we see the damage that these vehicles do. Some people show no compassion or respect for our hard work, or maybe they don't even realize the work that goes into getting a field into operation."

Q: What are you most proud of in life?

A: "I'm definitely a proud sixth-generation farmer. I'm very proud of how hard my parents worked to keep the farm going, in good times and bad. I'm also a very proud mom. I love to see how Ryan shows love for the farm, too, and when he leaves his day home he says to his friends "Guys! I'm going to the farm!" It just fills my heart with love!"

Q: For grain farmers, harvest is undoubtedly the busiest time of the year. How are harvest meals managed on your farm? (If you're not a grain farmer, pick an equally busy time of year on your farm and describe how meal times are managed.)

A: "Our busy time is what we call "hay time," which in Newfoundland is usually late June into the middle of July, and again in late September. Depending on the weather that year, we can sometimes squeeze in another cut between those months. We farm 600 acres, and we go as far as a thirty-minute drive to get to our fields. So usually myself or Mom will have pizza or subs (or whatever the boys want for that day) ready for when they get back to the yard with a load of silage. The first truck will take the harvester operators' lunch, along with the mowers' and hay rakers' lunches, to the field, and they will eat theirs in the field. We try to get it as close to supper time as possible, but sometimes it isn't until 10 pm that they get their supper."

Q: As you know, the demands of farming on your spouse's time is often such that they cannot contribute as much to home or childcare needs as spouses who work forty hours per week can. Describe how the never-ending task of housework is managed in your home.

A: "Before we had Ryan, I was working flat out six days a week, so I would just do a little bit each day. I found, too, that we would have my siblings and cousins over to our house at least 2–3 weekends a month, so that was a great way to MAKE me get the house cleaned up, haha. But now with Ryan, it's totally different. I read in a book once that cleaning up after a toddler is much like cleaning up after a party that you've never attended, and boy is it true! And I swear my little boy likes NOTHING tidy! I'll line up his superheroes or tractors, and as soon as he sees that, he DESTROYS it! So I've learned that it's a lost cause. I've also learned that its okay for the house to look like it's been lived in, haha. So it may not be the tidiest all the time. My mom, on the other hand, she can make my tidy look tidier, if that's even possible! That's when you know that she's been to our house to help us clean."

Q: When it all just seems too much (life, responsibilities, the juggling act) what is something you do for self-care?

A: "I'm definitely not the most "girly girl," so I'm not into getting my nails done and being pampered as such. But I do enjoy a cup of tea every evening right after Ryan goes to bed, which my husband will make for me, I might add! I also enjoy my exercise class that I do twice a week. It's called boxercise and involves fast music that you do boxing moves too. And I occasionally enjoy a few drinks with my family and friends, whether it's a night out with my girlfriends, or a gathering at one of my siblings' or cousins' houses. So I make time for these things a few times a month. What are we working for if we can't enjoy life a little bit more from time to time?"

Q: Having our families eat nutritious meals is becoming more and more a priority for families. Spending less time in the kitchen to achieve that, however, is also a necessity. What is a GREAT recipe your family can share that achieves both of these goals?

A: "We use our Crock-pot a lot. Especially where we are gone for a long time during the day. I just throw in the meat, and all the veggies, and it's all ready for when we get home. We also enjoy family barbecues weekly. It's nice to be outside and watch the kids running around while getting supper ready. Mom's pea soup is my favourite. I haven't attempted that one yet, though."

MAMA'S PEA SOUP

1 bag yellow split peas (soak in cold water overnight)
1 onion
2 pieces of salt meat (or hambone) cut into small portions
6 cups of water
6 potatoes
4 carrots
3 turnips

Cut vegetables into small, soup-sized pieces. Bring peas and water to boil and turn stove to simmer. Let simmer for 2–3 hours until peas have rendered out. When ready, add salt meat, potatoes, carrots, turnips, and boil until vegetables are tender. Serve with warm homemade bread or rolls.

(Photo: supplied)

Age at this writing: 33

Rachel Jensen lives seven miles northwest of Dauphin, Manitoba, with her husband and one son. Despite living and working in other places at various points, for thirty-three years Dauphin has been "home." She has been married to Jens for nearly six years and their son, Nicholas, is two and a half. Although, I don't know her overly well, I am related to Rachel through marriage. From what I do know of her, I was eager to interview her and learn more about her life on their farm.

Q: What does the term 'farmwife' mean to you, and do you consider your-self to be one?

A: "I admit, when I hear the term farmwife, my mind instantly goes to the stereotypical vision of a woman in the kitchen, making meals every day, raising the kids, cleaning, doing the books, tending the garden, canning, milking cows, etc. In this definition, I'm not a fit, that's for sure! Although I do still do some farmwife-y duties, I also run every piece of equipment the guys do, clean bins, service equipment, think about and analyze capital purchase needs, and communicate and negotiate with service providers. I think it's important to start think-ing of the term farmwife with less of a paintbrush. I am just like most other wives out there, managing the balance of work, kids, activities, community, and life—with running a business in there as another ball to juggle!"

Q: What was your background prior to marrying your husband?

A: "It was a combination of working, school, and travel. After high school, I made it through a year of university then decided to put that on hold. So I spent a year in Whistler, British Columbia, living, working, and snowboarding. I had to find a summer job there because I didn't have the money to make it home for the summer! So, with $32 to spare, I went tree planting in BC. I made great money because I worked hard, which funded my travels to Australia the two years following. I lived and worked on several farms there. When I decided to go back to school, I continued tree planting, which helped me get through school virtu-ally free of student debt, and I could be home for harvest in August. By 2009, I had completed an Agriculture Diploma at Lakeland College in

Vermilion, Alberta, an Ag-Business Degree with Great Distinction from the University of Saskatchewan, and had started to get jobs in the Ag industry closer to home. Jens and I both had our own separate farming operations before we were together in 2009. I finished my degree then managed to land a job in Dauphin, Manitoba, that fall. We started running our farm together in 2011 before we were married, and bought land together that year too."

Q: Briefly describe your family farm business and its key players. If you have a business or career "off the farm," tell me about that, too.

A: "The family farm as a whole crops 5,200 acres. We grow a fun mix of your typical cash crops (canola, wheat, soybeans), perennial crops (timothy, fescue), and specialty crops like hemp and corn. There are four families involved in this operation: Jens and I, my parents, and my two sisters and their spouses. Each family has their own land base (Jens and I farm 1,200 acres in our "sub farm"). We all share the labour needs, especially at harvest time, and we all pay my parents' corporation for custom work. All us "kids" have off-farm careers, so most of the day-to-day work is done by Dad and Jens, with me and my brother-in-law around evenings and weekends as much as we can. Jens has his own woodworking shop, so his time is a bit more flexible and he can be available to work on the farm during the growing season.

I have a full time off-farm career in the financial services industry where I've been for over seven years. I managed a branch of the local credit union for a couple years, which was great leadership experience. I've gone back to a lending role with the CU now, which is a bit more flexible for holiday time during harvest. My off-farm career has provided experiences and is developing a skill set that would have been impossible to achieve working on the farm alone. Learning how to manage changing situations, lead people, and work with people effectively are important skills to have when working in a team or running any business, farm or not. How we work with other people has a huge impact on our farming business and my job has definitely helped me to develop in this area. It sounds simple, but it really took me years to figure it out!"

Q: What do you consider your primary role?

A: "I know what I SHOULD say to this question ... that my primary role is to take care of my family and be a good mom, but honestly, I have to say that my primary role is to balance and organize three primary roles—mother, career woman, farmer—and do so effectively every day. One is not necessarily more important than the other. There are times I want to just hang out with Nicholas and play but that field needs spraying or a customer needs something last-minute so I have to work late at the office. I need the farm and my career to create a good life for my son, and in doing that, I think I am being a good mom. I just need to show him that hard work and a high give-a-shit factor for what you do every day is very important, while not forgetting to pick him up from day care!"

Q: Has there been anything in your family or farm life that you've wanted to change?

A: "If I could change one thing about our family and farm business it would be to communicate more openly about the tough stuff like the "worst-case scenario." While I think we are doing better than lots of family farms in my working experience, we have farther to go!"

Q: On some Canadian farms where multiple families are involved, there are a variety of land- and home-ownership complexities that still exist today. In terms of the ownership setup of your farm, is there anything that worries you about your own or your children's security?

A: "This is SUCH an important question! The topics of accident, death, divorce, illness, etc. so often get left behind because people are afraid to talk about them and the fact that there will be discomforts (likely true) in talking about the worst-case scenario. Of course we don't want the worst to happen, but we would not be protecting our family or business if we didn't consider it.

In our case, there are two areas to protect: the present and the future. The present ownership setup of the farm is pretty simple. We all own our own land base and farm our land bases separately. So individually we all know what our balance sheets look like and that's what we want to protect. What Jens and I have done to protect each other and our family comes down to three basic things: 1) Keep our wills up-to-date and reviewed by our lawyer and appointed executor at least every two years; 2) Have adequate life insurance coverage in place to pay off the term debts, provide a living for Nicholas till he's at least twenty-five, and pay for his schooling; 3) Review our business and estate intentions with each other and with our family— especially Nicholas' appointed guardians—regarding the worst-case scenario.

In my line of work, on the financial end, I have seen what can happen if none of these are done. I have also seen instances where all of them were done but the big missing piece was the conversation. Often there is an active and valid will but it gets contested because the family cannot agree on the intent of the person's wishes. That can be interpreted in so many ways! If families would just have a conversation so that the final wishes and plans for the business and the estate (which are two VERY different things) are made clear to everyone, then at least everyone would know where they stand if / when the time comes.

This is easy to do when it comes to managing something that is your own. Under joint circumstances where there are more families involved in the ownership of assets or shares, it can get complex. This brings me to our "future" concerns.

We don't know what the future involvement or ownership structure for our farms looks like just yet. The most important part is to talk about it and make sure everyone involved knows the intentions behind future plans. I will admit that this has not been discussed in depth or decided with the whole family yet, but my mom and dad have been working with the accountant and lawyers to develop a proposal of the main farm ownership for the future. It's easy to develop a plan for your own business and estate, but it is much harder to convince someone else that it's important to talk about theirs.

This topic has become more and more important to Jens and I over the last couple years. We have been doing more and more work on the farm and we have been growing our land base. We are at the point now that we need to know what the future intentions are for the main players so that we can work on some long-term plans of our own. I seem to have been bugging my parents every three months or so to get us all together to at least start talking about it, but there always seems to be an excuse to hold it off. This last summer, I saw three of my customers pass away suddenly. And I saw three families virtually get torn apart because no one talked about what would happen after "dad" passed away.

That's when Jens and I agreed that it was time to make our intentions known and to explain why talking about this is important to us, to them, to our family, and to the business. Here is what we did to make them talk to us about it:

We set up a meeting with everyone. We got a babysitter for the evening. We prepared an agenda and a PowerPoint presentation. The title was "Rachel and Jens' Intention Seminar."

Topics on the agenda included: What are our future intentions? Why do we want to be a part of this business? Why do we think we can add value? Why do we believe it is important to initiate succession discussions now?

We kept the focus on why these topics are important for us and at least it gave the family the opportunity to formally hear our intentions. We did not go into what we think they should do—that's up to them, and telling Mom and Dad what to do with their business is not something I think anyone should do. The idea was that we share our ideas and what we are prepared to commit to the business, which will encourage them to do the same.

As explained, there are four family operations involved in total, with the main farming corporation owned by my mom and dad. The question is what will it look like when Mom and Dad are looking to exit? The main farm is their business and they get to decide what they want to do with it in the future. The key here is exactly the same message as above: that the intent needs to be communicated to everyone involved so that we all know what will happen in this future scenario.

After our presentation, we made a commitment to a follow-up date to discuss a few questions that came up at the first meeting. We followed up with our answers, then we got them to commit to a time to have a similar intention-based conversation. We have been very specific around deadlines so that everyone is accountable to them. We are now working with a new deadline to discuss the final proposed plan that has been created by Mom and Dad and their advisors.

At least now we feel that the discussions that need to happen are starting to happen. We have deadlines in place and we showed some initiative and took a risk to open that door and show that we can get comfortable having these "uncomfortable" conversations."

Q: "What is a hilarious story you can learn about life on your farm?

A: "One fall, we had my cousin come and help us work on the farm. We got him started doing the easy fieldwork like harrowing and picking stones. One day he was pulling the harrows back into the yard and he got a bit too close with the folded harrow bar to a swing auger that was set up in the yard. The whole unit toppled over onto its side! It wasn't so hilarious at the time but it did lead to the new rule number one on the farm: Don't make work for Ernie! It's pretty funny explaining to people where that rule came from now.

There was also the time I was climbing up bins to check them and my ladder fell down. My cell phone was in a very useful place: down in the truck. After waiting for a couple hours (I guess no one missed me ...) I fashioned a "rope" out of my pants and shirt to get down to a safe level I could jump from. I had to explain to Dad what had taken me so long when I got back to the yard!"

Q: What are some ways you try to keep your marriage strong?

A: "We work together every day towards the common goal of running a successful business. Communication, communication, communication keeps us successful as business partners, which keeps our marriage strong. I am also lucky that he is easy to keep happy with a good cheesecake whenever I screw up and don't listen!"

Q: For grain farmers, harvest is undoubtedly the busiest time of the year. How are harvest meals managed on your farm? (If you're not a grain farmer, pick an equally busy time of year on your farm and describe how meal times are managed.)

A: "Harvest is definitely the time when our family comes together the most. My mom and older sister manage most of the meals, and the after-5 pm childcare for Nicholas most days too when I go out in the field after work. I am super-grateful for the help we get with Nicholas during the harvest season! When there are enough helpers around, there are days when I help with meals. This is usually last-minute, and mine end up being pretty simple! Rueben sandwiches, steak tacos, or B.E.L.T. sandwiches with fresh veggies or salad are my go-to ... or Subway! So I manage meals by keeping it simple and calling in reinforcements when needed!"

Q: As you know, the demands of farming on your spouse's time is often such that they cannot contribute as much to home or childcare needs as spouses who work forty hours per week can. Describe how the never-ending task of housework is managed in your home.

A: "For housework, this is managed in two ways during the summer: 1) It doesn't get done or 2) Call in the housekeepers! There are weeks that go by where we are just picking the clothes off the top of the "clean" pile, or I'm sweeping the floor at 1 am. Sometimes I will even take a secret half-day off of work that I don't tell my dad about to do housework. When harvest gets close, I have a cleaner come every week just to keep the floors and bathrooms clean. It's really nice coming home at midnight from the field and everything has been freshly cleaned! We are really lucky to have our neighbours' kid around to keep our grass cut for us every week. It's not unusual for Jens and I to shine the truck lights on the garden after getting home from the farm and do some weeding for an hour before going in!

For childcare, we are lucky there too! We have full-time day care and my mom helps with Nicholas a lot during the summer while we are working on the farm. We have a couple neighbour kids who babysit some evenings and on the weekends too, which helps. When I do have him in the evenings, he just tags along with me to pick up trucks, help move to fields, move augers around, or fuel up equipment. I can do all of that for a few hours with him safely in tow and it all helps the guys get a better start the next day."

Q: Having our families eat nutritious meals is becoming more and more a priority for families. Spending less time in the kitchen to achieve that, however, is also a necessity. What is a GREAT recipe your family can share that achieves both of these goals?

CHICKEN, RICE AND STEAMED VEGGIES

Chicken breasts
Club House Wet Rub Marinade of choice
Rice—white, brown, or whatever you prefer
Assorted veggies—whatever you have on hand. My faves are
   carrots, broccoli, cauliflower, bok choy, and celery.
Garlic (or garlic powder)
Coconut milk
Salt and pepper to taste

Use rice cooker for the rice. Add water and seasoning. Hit the 'cook' button for perfectly cooked rice in 15–20 minutes! No boiling over. No burnt mess on the bottom of the pot. I like to make a brown and wild rice blend cooked with coconut milk and salt.

Use meat tenderizer to flatten out the chicken breasts. Taking 5 minutes to do this helps the chicken cook faster and evenly. Slather the chicken in a Club House Wet Rub Marinade. Grill on Med–Low heat 5–7 minutes per side, or bake in the oven.

While the chicken is cooking, heat vegetable broth with minced garlic or garlic powder and pepper in a hot wok. Throw in carrots, cauliflower, broccoli, peas—whatever veggies are on hand. Keep wok covered and the steam from the broth will help cook things super-fast. The broth adds great flavour without butter or oil!

An awesome, tasty, healthy dinner in 20 minutes!

Tips for dessert: I make either a cake or a batch of muffins / cookies every week. Pack them for lunches and they're also good to have on hand for last-minute desserts!

INTERVIEW #24: Irmgard "Irmi" Critcher

(*Photo: supplied*)

Age at this writing: 56

Irmi comes to us from the British Columbia Peace River region, between Dawson Creek and Fort St. John. She was recommended to me by several women when I made the "callout" on social media for BC representation for this book. Irmi has been married since 1982 and has lived in Peace River Country ever since. She and her husband have three grown children.

Q: What does the term 'farmwife' mean to you, and do you consider yourself to be one?

A: "I guess I am a farmwife, but not in the traditional sense. I consider myself more like a business partner. I did all the typical farmwife things, where you raise your kids and grow your own vegetables, but I was never the person to go to quilting groups or exchange recipes. I ended up getting more into farm politics; I sit on male-dominated boards with local and provincial producer associations."

Q: What was your background prior to marrying your husband?

A: "I grew up in a village in Bavaria, Germany, on a small farm. I went to a college in Munich, where I finished my diploma in business administration, specializing in commerce and foreign trade. I had landed a job, but prior to that I wanted to travel, so I decided to take a leave of absence and backpack through Canada. I ended up on a farm in Northern BC where I met my future husband. He had just started his stint on the same farm as an agriculture exchange student from the UK!"

Q: Briefly describe your family farm business and its key players. If you have a business or career "off the farm," tell me about that, too.

A: "Barry and I basically ended up immigrating to Canada and starting a farm of our own in the area where we first met. We initially wanted to go into livestock (he comes from a dairy farm in south east England) as this was his area of expertise, but we ended up going into crops and starting a custom work business. This got us started in Canada. We have since dropped the custom work and expanded into a full grain farm. We now farm about 4,000 acres and we grow wheat, barley, oats, canola, peas, and grass seeds. We incorporated our farm about fifteen years ago and Barry and myself are the decision makers. Our son is now employed on the farm. I initially worked off the farm as an office manager on a big ranch nearby but when baby number three came along, I stayed home full time."

Q: What do you consider your primary role?

A: "I still do the bookkeeping and manage the finances of our business. My role has shifted a bit, from working alongside my husband to more office- and management-orientated work. I still help out outside, but more as a filler rather than it being my responsibility."

Q: On some Canadian farms where multiple families are involved, there are a variety of land- and home-ownership complexities that still exist today. In terms of the ownership setup of your farm, is there anything that worries you about your own or your children's security?

A: "As we were building the farm it was pretty straightforward; we both had the same goal and we worked together to achieve that. Ownership was joined and our accountability was only to each other. While it is nice to have the children interested in farming, the complexities come when there is only so much land base to go around. Also the son is still considered the primary person to take the farm on; however one of our daughters has furthered her education in agriculture and also has a husband who is a farm boy. They are both working off the farm but are interested in joining the farm. This is a bit of a dilemma as we need to figure out how to provide opportunities for the next generation, yet guarantee that we have a financially secure retirement, without crippling the farm's financial viability. As we are transitioning into a succession plan I wish my kids would make sure that they can get along so as not to jeopardize the farm's viability and the family's harmony, realizing that fair isn't always equal!"

Q: What do you think is a key lesson we can learn from the older generation of farmwives, and what is a great piece of advice you've been given from the older generation that you've valued?

A: "I had some neighbour ladies who were a generation ahead of me and they were good farmwives, helping their husbands out wherever they could, sewing their kids' clothes, gardening, and also known for their hospitality. As I was very young when I came to Canada, I had to learn a lot; in a way I was completely out of my comfort zone. One of these women helped me a lot by teaching me all the necessities of what it takes to live on a farm and be self-sufficient, but also that it is okay to put up boundaries—you can't be a wife, a mother, *and* a full-time hired guy!"

Q: What is a hilarious story you can learn about life on your farm?

A: "Our Hog Rodeo. I wanted to be completely self-sufficient and raise our own meat by having chickens and pigs, so we bought a bred sow. We had an old barn that came with the farm. It was in need of repair; nevertheless we housed the pregnant sow in that barn. She didn't show very much but was supposed to have the piglets any day. I was hoping it was going to be before my in-laws from England came visiting. Well, the visitors came and still no piglets.

One morning, my father-in-law went to check on the pig to see if she had had them. He went into the barn but the sow was gone! Big panic. Where was the pig?! The whole family started looking all over the yard and the bush across the road.

Evening came, and still no pig! We realized it had pushed against the door, slipped through a gap, and run off. Next morning, still a bit mystified, we heard some snorting noises outside; sure enough, the pig was rooting around in my flowerbed. She had come back! She looked a little worse for wear and it looked like she'd had her piglets, so off we went again trying to find the piglets, but to no avail. We could not tell if the sow had had the piglets or perhaps was never pregnant in the first place.

The in-laws' trip was close to the end and since there were no piglets, the pig had to go; no use feeding it if there was no offspring. My in-laws thought it was a good idea to help me get the pig to market, so we fixed a crate on the back of the pick-up, made a little chute up to it, and opened the door thinking she'd just climb up there.

Right! That didn't go exactly as planned. The pig must have known something was up, and as soon as my father-in-law opened the door a crack to let the pig out to the pick-up, she took the opportunity to make a run for it right between his legs. He caught a ride on the pig, backwards across the lawn, just like in a rodeo! Pam kept shouting, "Mike, hold on! Hold on!"

Finally he couldn't hold on any longer and took a nosedive onto the ground, the pig squealing and running off! The look on his face was priceless as he got up and dusted himself off! "Blimey, that was a hell of a ride!"

We laughed so hard, and he sure had a story to tell when he got back to England about his pig rodeo in Canada! We eventually got the pig caught and sold at the auction. We took quite a loss on it and never had any more pigs on the farm after that."

Q: What are some ways you try to keep your marriage strong?

A: "By showing interest in what he is doing and going through, and getting him talking about it (guys tend to be tight-lipped). One of our favourite things to do together is crop checking; we can spend time alone, look at the crop, and talk about the big picture (or anything else that is on our minds at the time)! We also like going away on holidays together often. We share a lot of the same interests—hiking, paddling, snorkelling, camping—and we recharge ourselves and our marriage when we do those things."

Q: What are you most proud of in life?

A: "I know I am supposed to say my kids, but I like that we built a farm up from scratch, that we raised three responsible adults, and stayed happily married through all of this!"

Q: For grain farmers, harvest is undoubtedly the busiest time of the year. How are harvest meals managed on your farm? (If you're not a grain farmer, pick an equally busy time of year on your farm and describe how meal times are managed.)

A: "When the girls were old enough—about 11 or 12—they had to do the cooking and send it out with one of the trucks. When the kids went off to college we just packed bigger lunches and skipped warm suppers. Now that we have a bigger crew, we get either our daughter or the wife of one the guys helping us to do the meals; I am usually in the field with the guys so I don't have to worry about it, other than planning what needs to be done at home."

Q: As you know, the demands of farming on your spouse's time is often such that they cannot contribute as much to home or childcare needs as spouses who work forty hours per week can. Describe how the never-ending task of housework is managed in your home.

A: "During the years when my kids were small I usually did most of it. As the kids grew older, they had to help a lot. Schedules were made up of who had to do what, and it got done! They still talk about it how hard they had to work (not really). Now that the kids have moved out (but are usually here on a daily basis) my husband shares the cooking, helps with a thorough clean, and maybe even throws the odd load of laundry in. I really like it when he cleans because he is way fussier than I am."

Q: When it all just seems too much (life, responsibilities, the juggling act) what is something you do for self-care?

A: "I like having some alone time. Especially when I went to meetings a lot, I would usually arrange my travel so I had some spare time while I was there to either go shopping or meet up with friends and go for dinner, or go for a long walk or even a spa appointment."

Q: Having our families eat nutritious meals is becoming more and more a priority for families. Spending less time in the kitchen to achieve that, however, is also a necessity. What is a GREAT recipe your family can share that achieves both of these goals?

A: "In the summer we do a lot of barbecuing usually accompanied by a big salad, anything that grows in the garden. Grilled veggies in olive oil with herbs are a favourite. I don't really have a recipe, I just use what I have at home. It all tastes good."

Looking to the Future: Food for Thought

Farming is complicated. Farm life is complicated. That's why I've included this section with input from professionals who have graciously lent a little of their expertise.

None of this information is intended to provide actionable "advice," rather I've compiled this supplemental information to help inspire you to educate and inform yourself based on your own situation.

Brenda Albers, a Wealth Protection Specialist with Servus Wealth Strategies and Servus Insurance Services, offered the following information with regard to farm women specifically:

INVESTING

A stay-at-home mom does not have the opportunity to earn an income independent from the farm. The farm accountant will calculate the farm net income after taking advantage of every allowable tax concession that the government permits. This usually results in a very low personal income for income tax purposes, leaving very little room for Register Retirement Savings Plan (RRSP) contribution. Allowable contributions are determined by an individual's personal income amount.

A stay-at-home mom can consider saving money in a tax-sheltered environment by using the Tax Free Savings Account (TFSA). Every Canadian resident who is at the age of majority, which is 18 or 19 depending on the province of residence, is eligible to make contributions. The maximum contribution amount for 2017 is $5,000.00. If you have never made a contribution, you can make up past amounts to a combined contribution maximum of $52,000. The TFSA can also be used as a place for children to save money for their future expenses, such as education, buying a family home, buying farmland, etc.

Other savings plans include the RRSP and the Registered Education Savings Plan (RESP). It is advisable to speak with a financial planner to determine which plan or plans would be best suited for each individual.

ESTATE DOCUMENTS

It is important that estate documents are current and in good order. There are three estate documents: the Will, the Power of Attorney, and the Personal Directive. The Will deals with a person's affairs upon death. The Power of Attorney is a document that allows a third party the right to act financially on an individual's behalf should they become mentally incapacitated and unable to make sound financial decisions. The Personal Directive is the document that addresses issues related to medical care, such as life support.

Estate documents need to be revisited and / or adjusted whenever a major event occurs. Major events can include marriage, birth, divorce, death, or any other event that may be considered important or relevant to the owner of the documents.

PROTECTING YOUR ASSETS

In the farm community it is very common for the family farm to pass down from one generation to the next. The farm will most likely stay within the spouse's family in the event of a divorce or death. Prenuptial Agreements safeguard spouses who marry into an intergenerational farm and later divorce. Life insurance financially protects the farm in the event of a premature death. Life insurance ensures sufficient monies to look after both the spouse who marries into the farm and the intergenerational farm stakeholders.

HEALTHCARE PLANNING

A farm family should have adequate insurance in place to address medical issues. There are several insurance companies available in the market to assist farm families with healthcare benefits such as Health and Dental

Care insurance, Disability insurance, and Long Term Care insurance. Health and Dental Care benefits cover the day-to-day dental care and medical prescription costs. Disability insures income in the event a person becomes disabled and is not able to work. Long Term Care insurance is used to assist in medical costs as farmers age into their senior years.

TRANSFERRING THE FARM TO THE NEXT GENERATION

We have all heard stories of farm families torn apart by farm transfers after the farm patriarch or matriarch passes away. Sometimes the way the farm is willed is a complete surprise to the survivors. If succession planning is discussed with the family ahead of time, they will be prepared and in the end more likely to maintain a good family connection. A good estate plan will help transfer the farm in the best possible fashion while keeping the family unit intact. In some cases, life insurance can assist in equalizing the estate, creating fairness amongst the heirs.

Elaine Froese, is a Farm Family Coach, Speaker and Succession Planner from Boissevain, Manitoba. She has more than twenty years experience working with farm families and she offered this:

Work / family time, in other words work / life balance is an unresolvable problem in that it has to be managed daily, and so is never "solved." It's a polarity that causes huge stress and tension when there is confusion about roles or unrealistic workload expectations. Women tend to add more to their list without subtracting or practising good self-care. Does the farm serve the family (which is healthy), or does the family serve the farm?

Debt servicing causes financial stress. Families often depend on off-farm income to pay debt and earn too little net income from their off-farm and farm income. Farm women tend to be well educated, yet they and their spouses may not be getting a fair wage from the farm to give the family disposable income to service debt. Farmers also neglect developing a "personal wealth bubble," which puts strain on the transition / succession plan and financial cash flow.

Conflict avoidance and procrastination are the underlying issues that hold families hostage. The in-laws dynamic, fear of dce, the inability of founders to let go all become "un-discussible," and the lack of written agreements to create certainty for everyone's future wellbeing creates tension and provides no resolution.

Farm women risk their security by not being aware of their financial status and not having a voice in the decision making.

Be financially smart and speak up. Ask for what you need to know.

www.elainefroese.com

Stephanie L. Dobson, BA, JD, is a Registered Collaborative Lawyer, Registered Family Mediator (specializing in parenting and divorce), Registered Parenting Coordinator, and Arbitrator from Meridian Law Group of Lloydminster, Alberta.

When we start out cohabiting with someone and even when we marry them, we don't often want to think of the "what ifs" of if the relationship were to break down. We think of the partnership, of building a life together, having children together, and being a family. In the context of farm families, the venture of farming truly is a joint effort, and there is often a division of labour that exists out of necessity rather than out of a desire to perpetuate a stereotype. It can be a very rewarding life building a farm together—growing the operation, raising farm children, working together with extended family to continue the growth. But what happens for the farmwife when a marriage or cohabiting relationship breaks down?

The laws of property division are provincially regulated, and therefore it is impossible to provide legal information that would be universally applicable throughout Canada. However, there are some general considerations of which all farmwives should be aware, in the event that divorce should come upon their family.

Upon marriage breakdown, spouses are entitled to divide the assets and debts owned by either or both of them. That means that even if your name is not on the assets, you will still be entitled to a 50 percent share in the total net worth between you and your spouse. This extends to all farm assets such as land, equipment, inventory, livestock, buildings, etc. In some provinces, this right extends to non-married cohabitating spouses.

One major consideration, though, is that many provinces have something called "exemptions." Two main areas affecting farm families are exemptions relating to 1) inheritances / gifts and 2) assets brought into the marriage. Usually, the value of assets that existed at the date of marriage are not considered "shareable" on divorce, but any increase in value may be shareable (depending on your province). For instance, if land owned by your husband at the date of marriage was worth $300,000 and by the end of your marriage it is worth $500,000, then the shareable portion of the asset is only $200,000 (the increase); at 50 percent, you would be entitled to $100,000. If your provincial laws recognize exemptions, this principle would extend to any inheritances / gifts / items brought into the marriage, both farm-related and otherwise.

It's advisable at the start of the marriage / cohabitation to make a list of assets / debts and their values. It is amazing what time can do to one's memory, and in the event of marriage breakdown spouses are often left trying to recall what was owned at the start, and its value. That list would help reduce conflict between you and your husband, as it would be clear as to what items should be in the pot to be divided.

What if you and your spouse are living on land and in a home that are not owned by you or your spouse, but rather by other extended members of the farm family (in-laws, etc.)?

Unless there is an agreement between you / your spouse and the owners, you may be seen by law simply as renters in the house / on the land, and it is possible that no ownership rights apply; in that case, your residence would not necessarily be a divisible asset. In order to counteract this, it's advisable to enter into a written agreement with the land / home owners to set out the intentions, if any, of an ownership transfer. Otherwise, be cautious about spending money on renovations or otherwise investing in the property.

Creativity is often required to arrive at resolution when it comes to the division of property for divorcing farm families. Typically farms are asset rich and cash poor. If, for instance, the divisible portion of a farm is ultimately valued at $5 million, it is unlikely that a farm could sustain the payout of a $2.5 million lump sum. To do so would likely cripple the operations, require the sale of assets, and threaten the sustainability of the farm for the traditional hand-down to the next generation.

If divorcing spouses are unable to agree, then a court may simply order the sale of assets to facilitate the required payout. If you and your spouse are willing to work together to arrive at resolution, then a solution that focuses on estate planning and / or payments by instalment to the other spouse can occur. Would you be willing *not* to take 50 percent of the value if you were reassured that your children would be given part of your 50 percent in assets as inheritance? Would you be willing to accept receipt of monthly payments over the long-term if it meant foregoing a big lump sum in your bank account?

The challenges for farm families going through divorce can be significant. Divorce could mean the loss of a business, a way of life, and a family system that goes back generations. How does a farmwife respect this history for their children's sake while ensuring that her rights are preserved and that her future is also secure? Farmwives are an essential part of making a farm prosper, and it is important that that role not be overshadowed by what is traditionally considered the main labour, borne by the husbands.

When Things Fall Apart: A Farmwife's Story

REBECCA KING

No one can prepare you for the loss of your spouse. This next interview is with someone very important to me. She is not only a very close friend but also someone who embodies strength, grace, resilience, and love.

Ever since 2011 when I first came up with the concept of this book, I knew I would want my good friend Rebecca to be a part of it. I knew she would be the perfect example of a "younger generation" farmwife, in particular for those who think tradition no longer exists. Her role in her family and her home since I've met her is no less remarkable than those of the traditional women before her.

When I married my husband Dean, Rebecca and another friend of mine put together a recipe book for me for our wedding shower. It was touching not only because it was handwritten and carefully crafted, but also because to me it was a "nod" that I was going to be accepted into this community of farmwives.

For the years since then we have become closer and I have grown more in love with her family and in particular their three girls. Dean is the godparent to their middle child; he used to ride the school bus with Rebecca. The bond runs deep and I consider myself blessed to be within it.

As I became more comfortable with my life here and continued to grow closer to Dean's friends, it was getting to know Don and Rebecca that reassured me that we were truly going to have a great life. We jokingly talked about where we'd hang out when we retired ("PV Garage, or the Wheatie?"). I excitedly told them of my decades-long plan to create my own retirement home that would really revolutionize retirement homes (with the introduction of Newfie band Fridays for a start). Our lives and our futures looked perfect.

Until they weren't. On June 21, 2015, our lives were forever changed when our friend Don—Rebecca's husband and dad to Marti, Kennedy, and Hudson—was killed in a head-on collision while driving with their oldest daughter Marti on an Alberta highway. Marti (or MJ as she's known to us) was saved.

None of our lives have been the same since this loss. Our community has been forever changed; our friend circle has been irrevocably altered. This loss will always be present.

The gravity of this loss to Rebecca and their girls will be saved for the book that she is meant to write one day. I can, however, tell you that her strength and grace has shown her to be even more amazing to those closest to her than she was considered before.

I have to thank Becky for agreeing to provide this interview for all of us. She has lived through what is for many of us, our worst fear.

Rebecca Jean King

(*Photo: Billi J Miller Photography*)

Interview with a 39-year-old widow
(A damn hard word for me to swallow)

Q: Briefly describe where you live and your background prior to marrying Donald.

A: "I am proudly living on the King family farm south west of Kitscoty, raising my three beautiful daughters where their roots run deep. I moved to the farm in November of 1997, just three months after marrying my best friend Donald King. Prior to this, I was living in Lloydminster and attending the University Transfer program at Lakeland College. As a child I was raised on a large acreage near Paradise Valley, Alberta, where my three younger siblings and I learned the values of discipline and determination. From a very young age we worked hard a lot, and played hard when we had the time."

Q: What year did you marry Donald and how long were you married before he passed away?

A: "I married Donald on August 2, 1997. We were young, but we were oh so in love. We were married for 18 years, 10 months, and 19 days. This summer would have marked our twentieth wedding anniversary. Dammit, do I miss him."

Q: Briefly describe your farm business with Donald. Who were its key players?

A: "The day we told Donald's father we were engaged to be married, he decided he would move into Kitscoty and we were moving onto the farm. So, at the ages of 24 and 19, my husband and I began our lives together on the generational farm. Don's dad was always present: working, helping, and giving advice ... I think he was very proud that his only son was taking over the farm and doing a fantastic job. As the years went on our family quickly grew and Don's dad's involvement became less and less. So initially, the key players were definitely Donald as well as his Dad and I, but in the last few years our teenage girls have played important roles in the functionality of our farming methods."

Q: Describe your role as a farmwife.

A: "Being a farmwife is my dream job, and I think I rocked it! (At least that is what Donald would tell me *blush*). My role consisted of being Donald's "right-hand woman," as well as bookkeeper, beer drinking buddy, and listener. I enjoyed just listening when he needed to talk things out or vent, and I would offer advice or encouragement whenever I could and always remind him "Honey, we cannot control Mother Nature." We did everything together; although there were many times when I was tending our precious babies, the garden, yard, and house, preserving, and cooking meals while he was in the field, whenever possible we were doing things together. I would harrow, land roll, combine, haul fuel, but not so much the grain as that was his job. I got out of that one when I was pregnant and unable to reach the clutch as my belly was in the way. Grain went all over the hood of the truck ... oops.

I was most often the hold-this, hand-me-that, go-for-this person and I enjoyed just being beside him ALL the time—even if it meant banging my head on a seed boot while crawling under the air drill to make sure nothing was plugged up because then he was right there to kiss it better My favourite was riding shotgun together on the way home after a long day in the field, and the comforting feeling of just being together.

When I asked my 11-year-old what she thought my role as a farmwife was she said, 'To cook the meals and make sure Dad didn't miss his T.O.A.!!' Lol."

Q: What role did Donald play on your farm and in your family?

A: "Donald was a very sensible farmer; he never concerned himself with having the biggest or best equipment, he just took really good care of the stuff he had. The farm and his family were his life, he never wanted for anything else. He was the decision maker, the "let's do something" person all the time, even if the crop was in and the cattle were fed. Donald did everything on the farm; he was the manager, main operator, fix-it man, problem solver, go-to guy and comedian. Most importantly he was the most perfect dad a child could ask for. He always took the time for his girls even if it meant he had to shut down the air drill (to the eye rolls from fellow farmers) to go watch one of their ball games (and usually get rooked into umping). The crop still always got in on time; he was a family first fellow.

I was asked by the litigation lawyer in the liability case, which, after nearly two years, is in the preliminary process, to "List the amount of hours per week of household services / chores your husband did."

I said, "My late husband and I did EVERYTHING together, I assisted him outside, he assisted me inside, always. In terms of the above, he helped with the cooking and cleaning, did all the vehicle maintenance (my daughters and I have learned the hard and emotional way that we must check oil in vehicles now; that was never our job), yard and yard equipment maintenance, all household appliance maintenance, assisted in bookkeeping, and everything in between. All of our ongoing renovations still remain incomplete, as he was a "jack of all trades," and in the midst of some beautiful craftsmanship in the restoration of our home.

Hours? Constant. Some of the other questions I have recently been asked along with this one: Did you and your husband ever fight? Yes. Was there ever a chance of divorce? No. Were there any infidelities? No. (Are you kidding me?!) This kind of stuff I was not expecting or prepared for in the loss of my husband. It is all just so brutal and irrelevant."

Q: What did you "do right" in terms of planning for the worst?

A: "Most importantly we had up to date wills. In January of 2013, Donald and I developed a farm corporation and under the advice of our very genuine lawyer we went home and really discussed the what-ifs and how we would l like to see each other go forward if the worst happened. And so with a glass of red wine and a shot of scotch, we talked, discussed, debated, and concluded on some very difficult topics. I am thankful for that. We also attended some succession planning seminars and farm transition courses, which have helped me with some of my recent decisions."

Q: Going through what you've gone through in the past two years (at this writing), what do you wish you had done differently?

A: "Spend more time, more time, and MORE TIME.

Discuss often with extended family their feelings and intentions regarding the "what-if" scenarios, as families change and grow.

Not rely on handshake deals—get things in writing. Death changes people and you quickly find out those who are genuine and ready to help, and those who are fake or only around for a little while.

Get counselling / help sooner. Along with the grief and immense heartbreak came anxiety that would make me feel like I was physically choking and running out of air. I was pushed into defence mode early after our loss, which meant I had to divide my attention and as a result was not there for my girls emotionally as much as I could have been ... I was barely there for myself. I was so on my own, alone with all of this, alone for the first time in my life. There is no ideal way to help children deal with grief and loss, but there is help, and when they say they are ready, get it.

Take care of yourself, period."

Q: Do you have any words of advice for women marrying a farmer today?

A: "You are not just marrying a farmer, you are marrying a lifestyle. Be sure you understand that. Farming is hard work.

Some things you will need to know as a farmer's wife include:

When you are out helping in the yard with tractors and implements, if they rev the engine that means look at them!

There is sign language and farmer sign language. Learn to tell the difference, especially when hooking on, backing up, and pushing posts!

Learn to shoot a gun! I am a good shot and thank goodness, as I have had to take care of numerous magpies, a sick goat, a spraying tomcat, a racoon, and scare off a few coyotes ... no skunks yet, but I suspect I will have to someday.

When you first get the tour of the farm you will learn quarter sections and fields not by their land locations but by who homesteaded or owned it last. Be sure to take note of this so when you are asked to bring fuel to 'The Reid Place' you know where in the hell you are going!

Realize your cinnamon buns will never be like his mother's, so don't feel afraid to buy them at Cinnzeo!"

RHUBARB PIE

Fill pie shell with chopped rhubarb (about 2 cups). Mix together and spread on top:

1 cup brown sugar
2 egg yolks
1 tbsp. butter
1 tbsp. corn starch

Bake for about 35 minutes in a 350 degree oven. When done, beat the left over egg whites with1 tbsp. of sugar. Pour over top and bake till light brown. Best served with ice cream, of course.

Finale:
On Finding Home

I have unbridled love and respect for the tradition and deep roots of Canadian family farms. It has taken me a long time to find home. Now that I have, my husband, our daughters and the "home" we've made together are of ultimate importance to me. I am lucky to be raising children with the best person I can imagine, and I intend on caring for this family and treating it with the respect it deserves.

Despite all of the beauty farm life entails, I know that I'm not the only person who has married into this life with questions about how things can move forward in a more sustainable, progressive, and healthy way. I am convinced that we must educate ourselves on our own situations so that we can make the best decisions for our families, and our selves.

With that in mind, I wanted to take the veil off of the less romantic issues, for the purpose of giving farm women a voice and to inspire them to "arm" themselves with tools and knowledge. The ultimate purpose is to help strengthen marriages, families, and communities. I hope that my work creating this book, helps in some small way to do that.

Fair is fair.

Billi J Miller

Photo credit: Brin Dyer (www.be-photography.ca)

Age at this writing: 42

FARMWIVES 2

Q: Where do you live and how long have you lived there?

A: I live on a 107-year-old farm south of Kitscoty, Alberta (two hours east of Edmonton, Alberta). I moved here from Edmonton to be with who is now my husband, Dean in April, 2010. We were married later that year.

Q: How long have you been married, and if you have children, how many do you have?

A: Dean and I were married in October of 2010. We had our first daughter, Madeline, in November of 2011 and our second daughter, Kate, in July of 2013. We lost one during pregnancy, in between the two.

Q: What was your background prior to marrying your husband?

A: When I met Dean, I was living in Edmonton and working Monday to Friday in a career with the provincial government. I was single, had a great group of friends, and travelled every chance I got. I met Dean in August of 2009 through a mutual family friend, Charlie. Although a life with him was going to mean a very drastic change for me, I remember the choice as being an easy one. I haven't regretted it for one minute since.

Q: What does the term 'farmwife' mean to you, and do you consider yourself to be one?

A: I do feel like a farmwife in the sense that I am married to a full-time farmer and I believe when you are, you have a reality that is unique to that profession, just as it would be for a military wife, for example.

I don't, however, personally subscribe to the belief that when you marry a farmer it means that you automatically give up other professional goals or endeavours of your own. Women have fought long and hard for us to make our own choices.

I do not consider my primary role to be that of a traditional farmwife. I didn't take on all that was suggested that I do. If you are married to a full-time farmer, often, most of the childcare falls on you, so I accepted that priority while my children are in their preschool years. I didn't want to miss out on memories with my kids, so I don't fill my days with all of the other things many traditional farmwives once did. I come from a business background, so I value outsourcing some tasks for efficiency (the books can be done by someone far more qualified than me, for example; hair cuts can be done by a hairstylist; many young neighbourhood kids look for summer jobs and can help with the endless hours of yard work on farms, etc.)

Q: What do you consider your primary role?

A: I completely agree with my sister-in-law's answer to this question: my role is that of supplemental income earner. I have made the conscious decision in these early years of my children's lives to stay at home with them rather than pay for full-time childcare. That, in and of itself, is a full-time job.

In 2012 however, I also began my own business as a photographer and freelance writer. These two things are my passion. So, for the last five years, I have continued to build and grow that business with the intent that I will do it full-time when my kids are both in school.

Long story short: professionally, my role is that of business owner. Within my family, I am a wife and mom.

Q: What has your husband's role been in your family and on your farm?

A: His roles are: farmer, husband, and dad, and he is amazing at all three. He grain farms full time with his dad and one brother. They grow canola, wheat, barley, and peas. Dean also owns his own cows and operates a cow-calf operation. He is my partner in every way in our marriage and in our life together. He supports our family and encourages me in my goals. He is a loving, fun, encouraging, affectionate, hands-on dad and I am thrilled that my girls have that.

Q: Do you ever feel that being a farmwife takes away from any other personal goals you may have?

A: The only thing I feel I had to "give up on" by choosing this life was the ability to someday live anywhere else. Dean's life (and now our life) primarily focuses on this farm and this location. Because of that, we wouldn't be able to live elsewhere—at least not until retirement. I am completely okay with this now though. I love our life here.

Having said that, I do think that if I took on "all" the traditional roles that you could take on as a farmwife, very quickly my time to focus on any goals that I have personally or professionally would be zero. So, I don't let that happen.

Q: What is the best part, for you, in this life as a farmwife?

A: The best part of my life is the relationship I have to my husband and kids, and the fact that I get to do what I love and what fulfils me for a career. I love that we live on a farm that Dean's dad grew up playing on as a child himself. I love that I garden in a garden his grandma cared for. I love that I stare at a beautiful old barn built by his his family from my kitchen window. I love that the giant, towering spruce trees that line my laneway were put in the ground by Dean's dad and aunties when they were little, as they walked behind their mom. I love the roots here. And I especially love that my girls get to grow up feeling these same roots.

Q: How do you ensure you are not sacrificing your "self" when farm life and work is so time-consuming?

A: I literally schedule time in my calendar to take care of the things that keep me a fully functional being. I know myself well enough to know when I'm getting "off balance." My whole family knows when I'm getting "off balance," haha. If I do, I have no one to blame but myself, so I ensure I create time for what I need to keep happy: working on my business, taking care of our family, taking care of me, and a trip every now and then.

Q: What is the hardest part, for you, in this life as a farmwife?

A: I would say, like many of the older farmwives did, that taking care of the kids on your own at those times of the year when Dean is not home is really hard. I know it's necessary, however, so I don't fault or resent my husband for it. If it's an extra long harvest season, I do what I have to do to get breaks when I need them.

Q: Have you started any new traditions in your family that are important to you?

A: I'm sure that my husband would say I'm a real pain in the a** about this, but travel is important to me and I think it's important for children, so I prioritize taking trips together as a family.

My belief is that having that deliberate time together as a family without distraction is critical. Life gets busy and the farm is often all-consuming. I think it means a lot to the kids to have their dad around all day, every day for days at a time. Plus, you always come home happier and reminded of what matters most. Aside from this reason, I also think it's important for kids to learn about other ways of life than their own. I want them to be aware of what's happening outside of their two-block radius.

Q: Has there been anything you were not prepared for since becoming a farmwife?

A: I wasn't prepared for the frequency of the "open door" policy that applies when you live in a small, rural area. You could be coming out from a shower and there's someone sitting at your kitchen table waiting for you!

Q: Were there any expectations that proved especially difficult for you?

A: Had I assumed all of the roles of previous generations, I would find life extremely difficult. I also think that I would be unhappy in my life and in my marriage.

Since blending our lives, Dean and I have done a good job at making our family life work for the both of us. Our roles change based on what season we are in, but I think we do a great job of supporting each other. We are a good team.

Q: Has there been anything in your family or farm life that you've wanted to change?

A: Yes. I will speak openly about our personal situation for two reasons: 1) I know that there are other couples in this same (or very similar) situation, and 2) everything spoken about here has been discussed openly already between myself, my husband and his family. It is all said with the utmost of respect.

Dean has lived on this farm for twenty years. He moved into the house on the original homestead Fall of 1996. (There is only one house on the property and the yard is not shared). I have heard by many that it was apparently always his grandparents' wish that Dean live on this original homestead (I'm betting it's because of that "born-in-a-plaid-shirt" thing I told you all about earlier).

The property, however, is owned by Dean's parent's farm company. Despite this, Dean financed and built a shop on the property ten years ago and this is something we continue to pay for.

The home on the property (where we live) was built in the 1960's and it has required a number of costly upgrades for it to be a livable home. The money for this necessary work has always come out of Dean and my family income. We are now heavily invested into the property (on top of continuing to pay a loan paying for the shop).

Technically, however, our names are not on the title of this quarter, the shop, or the house. This causes me a million worries for all of the "what if's" that have been discussed in this book.

We are now (again) in the position where more home repairs are needed and instead of continuing to put a "band-aide" on them it is critical (to me, especially) that we find a permanent solution whether that be we build anew, or we undergo a suitable renovation. This is not something I am willing to do, however, without us owning our home.

It's important to me that Dean and I purchase the farm so that our investments finally belong to us and that we can properly protect our family. Had I known that nearly a decade after the fact, we would still be in this position, I would have advocated harder that Dean and I make a different choice for our family. We are now heavily invested and it appears that in order for our names to be on the title, a purchase is required and it is not yet clear whether this will be allowed to happen. This heavily affects our family's financial plan, not to mention: whatever work we do will be financed and the longer we wait, the longer it will take to pay off.

This situation has *by far* been the greatest stress in my marriage, and to me personally. My opinion is that it is a very big ask of a spouse (no matter what sex you are) to just assume that things will all work out as it should when such huge risks are taken.

Q: What is the most important thing you hope your children learn from farm life?

A: I love that my kids learn fundamentals like growing food, caring for and nurturing animals, about markets, and the way so many things work. At four and six, they know that "at seeding Daddy plants the fields; in summer we watch them grow; in fall he takes it off; in winter we sell it for the money we have to live on each year." They learn so many things about the natural world, like how various animals live, and predators versus prey.

Q: What do you think is a key lesson we can learn from the older generation of farmwives?

A: I had the luxury and privilege of writing an entire book on traditional farmwives, so I have been extremely lucky to learn a lifetime's worth of lessons from them. I think it goes without saying that they have passed down so much in their traditions, family values, work ethic, gardening skills, canning and food preparation skills, and so much more. But I think even more than that, they have taught us strength, resilience, honour, respect, and deep love.

Q: What advice would you give to women marrying into farm life today?

A: I can only speak from my particular perspective. My advice would be to have honest talks with your husband about both of your expectations in your marriage. For example, where you will live, whether or not your name will be on the land, whether or not you will become a company, and so on. Discuss with him honestly things that are important to you. Educate yourself on how farm business / succession plans will affect you. These things are important, and you do have a right to know. They are hard discussions to have, and you may feel that it is not "your place" to ask, but they are vital to your happiness and will determine your level of stress down the road. If you are going to make the right decisions for yourself and your family, you will have to know how these things will affect you. Also, educate yourself; don't simply rely on things just working out. You have a responsibility to look after yourself and your children.

Q: What are some ways you try to keep your marriage strong?

A: We take time for each other. Even if it's something small like sending him a text to thank him for something he did. Or, to tell him what a great Dad he is. Life can change in a minute and I don't want those important to me not to know how I feel about them. Talk, discuss, plan (thanks Becky). Family holidays away. It's important to spend time with your nuclear family and remind yourselves where the focus should be. Also, if you have amazing family like we do that enable you to take trips away alone together—do that! It's a great way to reconnect and have fun.

Q: When it all just seems too much (life, responsibilities, the juggling act) what is something you do for self-care?

A: I visit girlfriends. I have a group of six women who have been my best friends for more than thirty years. They know all my stories and are my sounding boards when I need them. Even if we can't get together, we have a very interesting WhatsApp text string going nearly twenty-four hours a day keeping us all up on each others' lives.

If I'm really stressed, I write it out. I don't journal, but I find if I'm having a hard time, writing things out helps (writing this book has been very therapeutic).

I think it's important to keep connected to your own personal goals and dreams. Don't lose your "self" in marriage and mothering. The stronger and more "whole" you are, the better it is for your marriage, and for your kids to witness.

Q: Having our families eat nutritious meals is becoming more and more a priority for families. Spending less time in the kitchen to achieve that, however, is also a necessity. What is a GREAT recipe your family can share that achieves both of these goals?

A: I have more "tips" than one recipe, per se.

1. I love one pot meals. Mostly because we don't have a dishwasher in this house, so the less dishes, the better!
2. When I'm in a real rush, I always have an Olivieri Tortellini package to cook with Alfredo sauce.
3. A SERIOUS game-changer for me has been Jamie Oliver's "5 Ingredients" cookbook. Check out the recipes online, or buy the book—whichever works best for you. But, truly—DELICIOUS food and only FIVE ingredients!

Q: What are you the most proud of?

A: I am really proud of my daughters and the relationship I continue to build with them every day. I am of course deeply proud of my marriage with my husband—he is honestly my best friend and I have so much respect for him. I feel like we keep getting closer and I am very happy for this. Also, I am proud of the goals I have accomplished in my life. I am motivated, driven and proud that I am showing my daughters to go after your goals.

Q: Do you have an app or "hack" that you use to keep yourself organized that you cannot live without?

A: My electronic calendar, synced to my phone. I'd be lost without it. Also, we have a big chalkboard wall in our kitchen that outlines our week. We love it.

Q: What is a hilarious story you can share about life on your farm?

A: When Dean and I first started dating, I was down for a weekend visit during harvest time. We were in a combine in the same field as his brother, combining peas. As we passed his brother Craig, we noticed a fire was starting behind him and his combine and spreading along the ground. Dean hurriedly grabbed his phone to call him and he yelled loudly, "You're starting a *&^%$%* fire!!! Get out of there &^%$#, there's a fire!" What Dean didn't know, however, is that he actually misdialled and called his dad, who was in another field standing by the bins. Poor Gary couldn't understand why he was being yelled at because he couldn't see any smoke anywhere."

My deepest wish for this book has been to empower all individuals to live as truly and happily as they are meant to.

To strong marriages, to healthy families, and to women—"the true hearts of the home".

- xo.

Closing Note:

** If you or someone you know are experiencing challenges in your life or on your farm that are negatively affecting your mental health—please reach out. Your mental health matters—call 911, or visit: www.suicideprevention.ca to find your local crisis centre.

If you are looking for information or resources please visit the "Do More Ag Foundation" at www.domore.ag. They are helping to champion the mental wellbeing of all Canadian Producers.

Acknowledgements:

There are so many people I have to thank for helping me bring this part two of a very long project to the light of day.

Thank you whole-heartedly to all of the women who have answered my questions in this book, whatever your feeling on the word "farmwife" is. Your stories have enlightened me, inspired and empowered me. I am tremendously grateful for your bravery in sharing your answers to the tough questions. This book would not be without you. Thank you from the bottom of my heart.

To the women I've requested professional contributions from: thank you for volunteering your time and expertise to offer insight into what is often confusing and difficult situations. My deepest hope is for women to arm themselves with knowledge and facts to create the very best lives for themselves and their families. You will help my readers do that.

Professional Contributors:

Elaine Froese
Farm Family Coach, Speaker and Succession Planner
www.elainefroese.com

Stephanie L. Dobson, BA, JD,
Registered Collaborative Lawyer,
Registered Family Mediator
Registered Parenting Coordinator, and Arbitrator
Meridian Law Group
Lloydminster, Alberta
www.meridianlawgroup.ca

FARMWIVES 2

Brenda Aalbers
Wealth Protection Specialist with Servus Wealth
Strategies and Servus Insurance Services
Edmonton, Alberta

Thanks to the Miller family for being open to having tough conversations of our own. Thank you from the bottom of my heart though, for being the grandparents that I always wished for my children to have. Your place in their (and our) lives is more meaningful than you know.

About the Author

Billi J Miller is a Writer • Photographer • Author and Speaker from east-central Alberta, Canada. Previously a city-living, 9-5 Government worker, Billi moved to the country to marry the farmer of her dreams in 2010. She found herself living on a 100-year old Canadian prairie farm that was thick with deep roots, and a long history. She is now a Mom to two girls, and the creator of her dream business where she writes freelance for newsprint + magazines, photographs families + landscapes, and is a published author. Miller has truly found her passion and has no plans to stop telling the story of inspiring Canadians. She resides with her husband and their two young girls on a 107-year old farm in Alberta, Canada where she works from her home office.

Follow Miller's Work

billi j miller
photography

www.billijmillerphotography.com

The Women Among Us Project
A Collection of Stories & Interviews by Billi J Miller
"Stories that connect • uplift • inspire"
www.thewomenamongus.com

"The Farmwives Book Project"
www.farmwivesbook.com

Follow her on Social Media:

Facebook: @billijmillerbooks
@billijmillerphotography

Instagram: @billijmillerphotog and
@thewomenamongusproject

CPSIA information can be obtained
at www.ICGtesting.com
Printed in the USA
LVHW01s1728280218
568183LV00001B/1/P